What's It Like, Living Green?
Kids Teaching Kids by the Way They Live

Jill Ammon Vanderwood
Cover and Illustrations:
Emma Austin

Booksurge www.booksurge.com

Library of Congress Control Number: 2009900172
ISBN: 1-4392-2477-3
Printed in the United States of America on 30% recycled paper
Cover and Illustrations by Emma Austin
Cover format: Clark Stewart
Book format: Jt Hollister

This book is dedicated to my granddaughter Autumn, my neighbor Nicole, my niece Azura and my sister Jeanette, who inspire me to get out there and make a difference.
JAV

Acknowledgments:
A special thank you goes to my husband Bill, who puts up with me and my passion for writing.
Thank you, Sara Fitzgerald, romance author for your her friendship and encouragement. Thank you, Emma Austin for sharing your talents, with your clever illustrations. Thank you, Tristi Pinkston for editing, and Jt Hollister, my trusted web designer and book formatter, from Why Wait Webs (www.WhyWaitWebs.com). Thank you, Clark Stewart for cover design.
A very special thank you to the green community and my contributing authors, who are the real experts in this book.

The purpose of this book is to bring awareness to kids everywhere of their responsibility for the earth. This includes the environment, the treatment of others, and the health of their own bodies.

Throughout this book you will find stories about families who live green, kids who are making a difference for the earth, and suggestions for things you can do to make a difference. You will find a quiz on how you live now. Take the challenge, and if you are able to make one step toward a greener lifestyle, think of the difference you can make for your planet and for your future health and well-being.

Table of Contents:

1
What's It Like, Living Green?

"Our actions speak much louder than words and we must be sure to walk with 'green' footprints if we wish for our children to follow in them."
Melissa Zenz

Living Green Quiz

1) Do you drink bottled water, or soft drinks?
A)   I use my own reusable water bottle, and
I use a refillable mug for my soda.
B)   I drink bottled water and soda several times a
day.
C)   Sometimes I drink bottled water and soda, but I
always recycle the bottles.

**2) What kind of bags do you use when you shop
at the store?**
A)   Our family uses paper grocery bags.
B)   We bring our own cloth shopping bags.
C)   We use plastic grocery bags.

3) How often do you eat at a fast food restaurant?
A)   We eat fast food several times a week.
B)   We eat fast food once or twice a month.
C)   Our family never eats fast food—we usually cook
and eat at home.

4) How do you choose products to buy?
A)   We buy products in large packages.
B)   We love to buy chips, puddings, and cookies in
small individual packages.
C)   We try to avoid packaged products as much as
possible.

5) Are you using water wisely when you shower or take a bath?
A)   Do you take long showers or fill the tub to the top for your bath?
B)   Do you only run the amount of water you need for a bath, or take a short shower?
C)   Do you keep the water running while you are doing the dishes or brushing your teeth?

6) How do you wash your clothes?
A)   I throw my favorite pants and shirt into the washer alone, so I can wear them tomorrow.
B)   I gather up laundry to make sure I have a full load.
C)   When I wash a small load, I run the washer on a low water level.

7) When do you run the dishwasher?
A)   We run the dishwasher after every meal.
B)   We only run the dishwasher when it is full.
C)   If we only need to wash a few dishes, we do them by hand.

8) Does your family use paper wisely?
A)   Do you take a newspaper?
B)   Do you often print emails and other things from the Internet?
C)   Do you use recycled paper sparingly and recycle or burn the paper after using?

9) Are you conscious of your water use?

A)   Do you water the lawn for hours every afternoon?

B)   Do you water two or three times a week, in the evening or early morning hours?

C)   Do you grow drought-tolerant plants and ground coverings that use less water?

10) Is your family using electricity wisely?

A)   Do you leave your TV or video game on because you plan to come back soon?

B)   Do you leave the lights on because you don't like entering a dark room?

C)   Do you turn off each light and appliance as you finish using it?

Environmentally Aware
Azura
Age 16
Albany, Ohio

Hello, my name is Azura. I have lived in the country with my mom and older brother for most of my life. We were brought up environmentally aware and taught to take care of the world around us. I am very appreciative of this and use this knowledge every day. Here are some things we do regularly:

Conserving Energy:

We turn the lights on only when needed. We watch very little TV, and watch DVDs on a low power laptop computer. We use energy efficient light bulbs and Energy Star appliances. In the summer, we don't use air conditioning. We rely on the shade from trees, keep the drapes closed, and the house closed up to keep the temperature down.

In the winter, our home is heated by an efficient wood burning stove with a catalytic converter, which cuts down on the use of fuel and emissions.

Since we use our electricity minimally, our maximum electric bill is only $14 per month.

Recycling:

Our family reuses plastic and paper grocery bags.

We use torn paper for fire starters, wash plastic bags to use again, and use grocery bags for trash. We use scrap paper for notes.

We fix things or have them repaired if possible rather than disposing of them.

Everything recyclable is taken to a recycling center and anything which is still usable, we take to a thrift store. We carpool or bundle trips, and now that I am sixteen, I learned to drive using my mom's biodiesel car, which burns reclaimed and filtered grease from restaurants. *(see the article in the reduce section). We also use a scooter for commuting.

The scooter runs on regular gas. It goes up to 40 mph, and gets about 80-90 miles per gallon.

Water:

We have a well on our property. We also collect spring water in bulk con-tainers, rather than buying small bottles, which we will have to dispose of.

We use our bath water to flush the toilet.

Our family hand washes dishes in large batches, with the sink full of water, rather than running the spigot constantly through the process. We allow the dishes to air dry.

Our spring is gravity fed, so no pump is needed. We have an underground tank in the woods that collects rain water/spring water. It is then filtered into a water pipe, which comes downhill to our house.

Eating Green:

In our vegetable garden we grow: green beans, soy beans, tomatoes, kale, chard, corn, basil, squash, dill, cucumbers, jalapeño peppers, and asparagus. We also have apple and peach trees. We bottle a good bit of our food from the garden and fruit trees each year.

Eating a lot of local fresh food from home or the farmers' market cuts down on fuel for transport.

Most of what we eat is local whole-organic and we buy in bulk, when possible, avoiding environmental toxins or excess packaging.

My advice to others is: We should all be aware of the waste we produce each year. We can try to reuse and even if we can't use it, someone else might be able to. People should recycle more to help cut down on all the trash.

A DARK GREEN FAMILY
Melissa Zenz from Florida
KidBean.com-Vegan Family Superstore

1.   **Above all else, we involve our children in our everyday decisions.** We have an open dialogue about what we buy, what we eat, what we wear, what kind of products we put on our bodies, what we do to relax, etc. In this way, we are able to introduce them to our thought processes and considerations for living consciously.

2.   **We teach them,** when age-appropriate, **about labor and environmental considerations for the products we do/don't buy.** My kids know to ask,

"Was it made in China?" And they know we will not buy it if the answer is "yes." They know we avoid plastics whenever possible. (The exception to this is when they want to use their own money. Then we leave the final decision to them.)

3.　　**We talk to them about our food choices and why we make them.** We are vegetarians and belong to a food co-op and buy from farmers' markets and farms directly. When at the supermarket, my children know to seek out locally-produced goods. We make charts of food, grouped by color, and talk about the nutrients in each. We enjoy having color-themed dinners (for example, "orange" or "green" night). In this way, they have been introduced to yellow carrots, purple potatoes, purple cauliflower, elephant garlic and dandelion greens, among others.

4.　　**My husband and I have been using canvas shopping bags for over twenty years.** My children have their own cloth bags.

5.　　**We spend a great deal of time in nature, much of it unstructured.** We enjoy long family hikes with our dogs. My children make crafts and toys from pinecones, sticks, leaves, flowers, rocks, berries, feathers and other natural objects they find.

6.　　**We talk openly about how our bodies work and what they need to function optimally and naturally.** For example, my children know a great deal about how white blood cells "eat" disease germs, aloe is a versatile healing plant, that certain foods contain dense amounts of protein that can help them when they're moody, and sometimes just being outside makes everything better.

7.   **We involve them in our activist efforts** including PETA, working to stop animal abuse. We tell them what we believe, but do not require them to share our beliefs, and hope they will grow up to be compassionate adults.

8.   **We have recently started composting.** My children help rake leaves, add lawn clippings, water the pile, mix the pile, and add ingredients to it.

We talk about what kinds of materials may be added to it (they especially enjoy the unusual ones, like pet hair and dryer lint). We all enjoy looking for worms and finding good food for them.

9.   **We catch-and-release insects rather than using pesticides.** When my son was about a year and a half old, he role-played the "bug removal" scenario frequently with a postcard and a small clear plastic container.

10.   **We grow some of our own food** and involve our children in all aspect of organic gardening. They especially enjoy harvesting and eating, but also help with weeding, digging, planting and watering.

11.   **We only buy recycled paper and recycle it again when we are finished with it.** We will soon be making our own paper out of the scraps from our children's art projects.

12.   **We have involved our children, from a very young age, in our recycling efforts.** They help rinse and sort containers. We learn about products made

from recycled materials and choose them over products made from new materials.

13.   **We make many of our own cleaning products** and involve our children in the process. They are learning to make various cleaners from ingredients like baking soda, vinegar, lemon juice and olive oil.

14.   **We run an earth-friendly, labor-friendly, vegan business (KidBean.com)** Our children help with tasks like counting inventory and putting shipping labels on boxes. We also talk to them about the kinds of products we carry, and don't carry and why.

15.   **We periodically go through all of our stuff** and sort out the clothes, toys, books, etc. that we no longer want/need. We then discuss what we should do with these things. In the past we have donated to Iraqi children and local homeless and women's shelters or traded items with other families.

16.   **We keep a bucket in our shower** to catch the warm-up water. We have a tank-less gas water heater, but it still takes some time for the hot water to get upstairs. We then use the water in the bucket to flush toilets, help fill up the washing machine, or water plants.

17.   **We choose natural and organic products for our pets** (five cats and two dogs). We use natural remedies for fleas, flushable wheat-based cat litter and organic pet foods.

18.   **As a family of four, we produce less than a 13-gallon trash bag a week.** Since we began composting, we now produce even less.

19.   **We reuse just about everything** we can as packing materials for KidBean.com. My kids regularly visit me in my packing area where I keep shredded paper and even used gift wrap from family and friends.

20.   **I think the most important way to start children out "green" is to just set a proper example** and

have open lines of communication with them. If, for example, they see their parents buying recycled paper and ink and printing on both side of the paper, or choosing locally-grown foods and fair-trade bananas, or buying organic cotton sheets and donating old clothes to a shelter instead of adding them to a landfill, they will be normalized to such actions. Familiarity breeds comfort and we humans are very much creatures of habit. Our actions speak much louder than words and we must be sure to walk with "green" footprints if we want our children to follow in them.

Aurora, Devan, Emily, and Lila
Northern California

Here They Are—the Girls of the Future!
Dotty Simmons
Simmons Naturals
Dinsmore, California (mailing address Bridgeville)

These are our four granddaughters. Every time we think of them, it reminds us how important it is to quit dwelling on the mistakes of the past, which have gotten us into the situations we face now, and put our energy into creating a future that will sustain these growing youth and their future families as well.

Our family tries to live consciously. That is, we try to be aware of the effect our actions will have on the world around us. There are so many levels to that, and we are always discovering new ones. While I suspect we will never quite think of everything, we shouldn't feel bad about doing the best we can. And people should always aspire to do better, always learning more about the connections between our actions and the environment.

> *"When one tugs at a single thing in nature, he finds it attached to the rest of the world."* - John Muir, naturalist, explorer, and writer (1838-1914)

We had the three older girls here for just over a week, and it was a good exercise in teaching them some basic green conscious living principles. It was a challenge for them, but they quickly mastered our crazy recycling system: burnable (newspaper for starting fires), compostable, recyclable (five categories), and what we call "Total Garbage." It was hard for them to remember to turn out the lights when they left the room. Hardest still was remembering that chickens do not get meat scraps or orange and banana peels. The dogs get the meat treats, and the garden compost, and worm pile get the others.

We use cloth napkins, and everyone has their special ceramic or glass cup that gets washed once a day or when needed. They helped me hang their clean wet clothes on our "solar and wind-powered clothesline."

The girls loved to gather the eggs from the hens and help us out in the garden. Not bad for a bunch of city girls. As their grandparents, we try to teach them where their food comes from. We also talk about birds and bugs and which wild plants are poisonous and which are edible, and why not to pick all the wildflowers in any one spot.

We cook with our granddaughters, everything from bread to pizza to energy bars, all from scratch. In our home, we do not eat anything that comes pre-made in a package. We drink cider they helped us press last fall.

We walk.

Grandpa and I can tell from their response that this is not all normal fare for them and that they love to see the connection between things—those little **"Aha!" moments where the dots connect and they see how one thing in life acts with another.** To see these connections is the first step toward living a conscious life that will sustain us into the future.

"We should try to be the parents of our future rather than the offspring of our past."
- Miguel de Unamuno, writer and philosopher (1864-1936)

A Homestead in the City
by Julie Mullin
North Carolina
Fiberactive Organics, LLC
www.fiberactiveorganics.com

When I was five years old, my family moved to a small horse ranch on the south side of Kansas City, Missouri. My parents loved horses, and this house came with a dark chestnut-colored pony named Little Man. He lived in a small paddock with a two-stall barn in the back yard. It was enough space for him, but not enough for Matt and Buddy, my parent's very tall strawberry-roan Tennessee Walking horses.

During the day we would ride them, brush their coats and tether them in the yard so they could cut and fertilize the grass just doing what horses do. At night they stayed in the paddock with Little Man. It was a workable arrangement, but my parents wanted all the horses to live at home, so Dad set about building a bigger barn.

Not too far from our new home was an abandoned neighborhood that had been built in the late 1800s. Some of the homes were bigger than others, but they still stood strong even after the occupants moved away.

Most people would say these spooky homes surrounded by overgrown vegetation were empty, but they were full of life: mice, squirrels, snakes, and even raccoons had moved in. **My dad made a deal with the** property owner—he would demolish the houses for them if they would let him salvage all the reusable materials. It was good for everyone.

We spent weekends in the old houses. My sisters and I knocked out plaster walls and ceilings while our father harvested load after load of lumber, nails, stone and brick. The largest of the homes even had a ballroom. My sisters and I pretended to be singers up on the stage or dancers, twirling around the ballroom floor. That floor became the floor of our barn. Heavy beams held up the barn roof and the boards that framed the houses' walls were sturdy dividers between the horse stalls. In all, Dad built four stalls with an overhang that sheltered hutches for our rabbits, which provided meat for our growing family. In the back of each stall were doors that led into a large feed and tack room.

It smelled good in our recycled barn, the warm smell of the old wood mixed with the scents of fresh hay, sacks of grain and the healthy smell of the horses' breath as they poked their heads over the half-doors waiting for their meal.

We stored everything in that tack room. We climbed on the barn's flat roof and played in the sun. My sisters and I spent sweaty hours cleaning manure from the stalls. Soon we had a giant manure pile that accumulated out front. What do you do with all that manure and old bedding? Start a garden, of course.

Most people don't know it, but compost made from horse manure is full of vitamins and minerals and makes the best-tasting tomatoes. Dad broke new

ground in the fall, so the soil amendments had plenty of time and moisture to decompose and be ready for spring planting. Rather than the clay soil of Missouri, which was good for making pots and bowls but nothing else, our soil was rich with fiber, carbon, nitrogen and the box of red wiggler earth worms Dad ordered from an ad in the back of Organic Gardening Magazine.

Dad grew all the staples an American family eats. He also liked to try interesting veggies he found in seed catalogs or seeds that friends or family members would give him. I remember Jerusalem artichokes, kohlrabi, parsnips and several varieties of lettuce. My meat-and-potatoes mother found these weird foods baffling. Dad liked trying new gardening techniques, too. One year he planted potatoes under a deep layer of old hay under some big apple trees; we ended up with loads of potatoes and as a bonus we got wheat from the hay. Dad ground the wheat in the blender and used it to make bread.

We had eight apple trees, two pear trees, two cherry trees and several walnut trees on our property. My dad not only gathered and grew our food, but he preserved it and did a lot of the cooking over the years.

I'm all grown up and have an organic garden of my own. Dad still puts out a little garden each year. The horses are gone, but a neighbor keeps him supplied with manure. That beautiful barn that was old, even when it was new, is pretty aged by now. There are a few holes in the floor and the roof sags here and there. But it still holds a lot, mostly memories of three little girls being raised on the bounty of a homestead in the city.

The Family with The Weird Bread
By Geoff Mullen
Age 16

First day of High School   Geoff Mullin August 16, 2006

I am the teenage son of a mother obsessed with saving the earth, starting in our backyard. Sometimes this lifestyle has its downside. Imagine what it's like taking a warm relaxing shower, only to be interrupted by the constant cries of "Get out of the shower, you're wasting water!" Or you get up from the TV or computer to the sound of, "You forgot to turn off the power strip, we're bleeding electricity!" It's a pain, sometimes, living with a rabid environmentalist. Though I love sitting by a warm fire on a cold winter night, I hate splitting and loading firewood, and get roped into it every year.

When I was little, we were known as the family with the weird bread. Some of my friends would eat before they came over to my house so they wouldn't get hungry while they were here. Others would bring their own food if they were planning to stay for awhile. Mom was always trying to get them to eat vegetables or something!

My mom enjoys raising endangered breeds of chickens and letting them free range in our two-acre yard. It's kind of cool, but, imagine my embarrassment when I took the guys into the backyard to hang out and Mom hollered, "Watch out for the chicken poop on the back porch." Another complication was the big sticks we always kept by the back door, because our rooster could attack you when you least expect it and you'd better be armed! On the other hand, showing my friends our green and blue eggs is always entertaining.

Yes, it's true, living green has been engrained in me from an early age, and I wouldn't have it any other way.

2
Recycle

**Oh, Mother Earth won't last long
if we don't all sing her song…
Recycle, recycle, recycle!
Jill A. Vanderwood**

Two Reasons to Recycle
Nicole Williams
Age 11
West Valley City, Utah

Nicole was nine years old when she started recycling. Her cousin Jody told her, "With all the beer your uncle drinks, you should start recycling cans." There are two main reasons Nicole recycles: "I take the cans to the recycle center to get money for them, and I want to save the environment." If she didn't recycle, Nicole says: "The cans would be put into the dump. The dump would get filled up faster, and I wouldn't have any money. Everyone should recycle paper and stuff to save the environment.

"My two uncles, my dad, a cousin, and my neighbor all save cans for me. They put them into a trash can that is set aside for only aluminum cans. I pick them up every one to three weeks."

Sometimes people will smash the cans and put them into large bags for her, but mostly, she has to sort and put them into bags herself. Some aluminum cans still have liquid in them.

Nicole says she doesn't mind getting dirty. She always needs a shower after working with her cans.

Nicole takes cans to the recycle center after she has at least twelve large bags, which is about every three months.

Around Christmas time last year, Nicole cashed in her cans, and was excited to get $36 for only five bags of cans.

Nicole used her money to get a present for everyone in her family.

When she had twelve bags in March, she got $76.84. She either saves the money or spends it on gifts and parties.

"If you don't throw away the cans, they can melt them down and make more cans. Then we won't have so many cans in the dump."

Just Put Your Cans
in the Bag By the Door
Autumn Debello
Age 9
West Jordan, Utah

Author's Note: This is written with and about my grand-daughter, Autumn.

I didn't start recycling until I was nine. I have a friend named Nicole, who kept bugging me every time she

saw me.

"When are you going to start recycling cans, Autumn?"

I kept telling my dad to recycle, but he never did. I also wanted to be in my grandma's book, hee, hee. She told me I couldn't be in the book unless I recycled. Finally, my grandma called my dad and told him all about saving the environment. He was surprised when Grandma told him how much money I could earn from recycling beer and pop cans.

She told him about my friend Nicole saving up her cans so she could buy Christmas presents for her whole family. I was listening to my grandma and crossing my fingers. I was so happy when my dad said I could recycle.

I made a sign to put on the trash can. "Put your cans in the bag by the door." It worked, and before I knew it, the bag was full. Each time I put a new bag by the door, it filled up too. *This is so easy,* I thought.

I live in two places, since my parents have joint custody. In Magna, where my dad lives, they don't have curbside recycling yet. I think they will have it soon if enough people complain.

In West Jordan, where my mom lives, they have had recycling bins for ten years—that's even older than I am.

Besides the regular trash cans, we have a blue recycle bin. We can recycle cardboard, newspapers, magazines, junk mail, tin cans, plastic bottles, and aluminum cans (but I don't put these cans into the bin, because I want to turn them in for money). Glass cannot be put into the recycling bin.

West Jordan even has another bin—this one is light green. The color reminds me of what goes into the bin—green grass and yard waste. I think it's a good idea too, so all of those things don't go into the landfill.

There are four reasons why I recycle aluminum cans: I want to save the environment, I want to earn money and learn responsibility. I also wanted to be in my grandma's book, so I could tell all the kids how easy it is to recycle.

The Davila Family's Recycling Program
Alexandra Gnoske Davila
President/Founding Member
RECYCLE ME Organic Cotton Clothing
www.recyclemeorganicstee.com

The Davila Family lives in a house on the north side

of Chicago, Illinois.

Everyone in the family helps with their recycling program.

"We've developed our own family program because we wanted to make sure everything we saved would be recycled and go back into the community," says Alix Davila, an avid recycle mom. Alix recycles, along with her three children, Isabella (6), Emma (5), Jack (2), and her husband, Hector.

Before the recycling even begins, the Davilas focus on reducing and reusing, the other two "r's" that don't get as much attention.

When they head out to the store with their cloth bags, the family looks for products with reduced packaging, that can be recycled, or already have recycled content in their packaging.

They like to buy fresh vegetables, rather than canned or frozen, skipping the plastic produce bags.

The Davilas prefer to buy items that come in glass versus plastic, because of the efficiency in the recycling process.

They buy milk and orange juice in glass bottles, because not only does it taste better, but the bottles can be returned. Each family member has stainless steel canteens to carry their water so they can avoid buying extra plastic.

"Because we look for other choices, our recycling containers have a limited amount of plastic," states Alix. "I still can't find ketchup in glass bottles, though." As for the other recyclables, the Davilas have also reduced the

amount of cans they purchase, since learning that most cans are lined with BPA, a chemical that can leach into the food.

The Davila family saves their recycling in plastic recycling bins and cardboard boxes, which they keep in their basement, for sorting and storing. About every two weeks, they pack the recycling items into the car and head over to the North Park Village Recycling Center, about a mile from their home. This center is part of a neighborhood community center that includes several buildings for community activities and houses The North Park Nature Center, an oasis for native plants and animal life.

When it comes to recycling, each member of the Davila family has their own assignment. Jack, being two years old, is in charge of putting the plastic recyclables into their container. Isabella and Emma, being older, are in charge of putting used papers into the proper container.

The girls are old enough now to help at the recycling center. Isabella gets to toss the glass jars, while Emma handles the aluminum. They share the job of recycling the plastic bottles.

Once the recycling is done, everyone takes a trip over to the Nature Center not only to appreciate the joys of nature, but to understand that the recycling they just did helped put money back into the Nature Center they get to enjoy for free.

What's their biggest challenge to recycling?
"The biggest challenge to our recycling effort is yogurt containers. My kids love their organic yogurt, but the hard plastic containers aren't recyclable. I'd love to see yogurt in glass containers!"

For the Davilas, the most important aspect of the recycling program is teaching their kids to think about

where things come from and being responsible for their choices.

"**When you start at an early age, reducing, re-using and recycling is what's normal, what's ac-cepted.** When I send my daughter to school with her lunch, everything comes back including the napkin! It's funny, because I never told her to bring back the napkins but she just knows that it can and should be recycled, not thrown away."

A family of five, the Davilas throw away two bags of garbage a week. "It's not perfect, but I remember when I was a kid, in a family of six; we would throw out at least one bag a day," says Alix. "Our next challenge is to develop a composting program and get our garbage down to one bag a week or less."

Devon's "Heal the World" Recycling
by Devon Green
devonshealtheworld.com

I was born on March 8, 1991, in Stuart, Florida. When I was five years old, a neighbor gave me a single bag of cans to recycle, and a junior empire was born as I started a recycling business that eventually would serve three counties in Florida. I liked the idea of finan-cial independence, so I started to ask other neighbors to save cans for me.

Since Martin County, Florida does not provide recycling services for businesses, the natural market for my recycling idea was the business community.

Since 1996, I have built my business to include over 100 customers as I learned about recycling and became a strong proponent of the idea. At the age of five, I coined the acronym "ABC's of Recycling" to help myself remember which metals Treasure Coast Recycling would take and recycle. A was for aluminum, B was for brass, C for copper, and S stood for stainless steel. This acronym has served me well as a teaching tool used to help others to remember these four important metals when I volunteer to tell others about recycling at community events.

From the start, I loved animals and wanted to use some of my newly found "wealth" to take care of them. I would go to the grocery store, buy cans of pet food, and donate them to the animal shelter. Very soon thereafter, I began to send some of my money to various charity organizations that cared for animals or had an environmental agenda like mine.

I volunteered my time for many charities and events including the Heart Walk, and I was named the top ju-

nior fundraiser for The American Heart Association for two consecutive years for raising over $2,000.00 for heart research.

Beginning at age five, one day each week, I took a ride in the family van, which pulled my recycling trailer. I visited nearly one hundred businesses and several residential customers and collected their empty aluminum cans and other recyclable metals. I turned in my collection to Treasure Coast Recycling, where they weighed the materials and paid me on a per pound basis. My next visit was to First National Bank, where I (1) deposited half of my weekly pay into my savings account; (2) donated thirty percent of my income to the local Humane Society, to my church/school, to the local children's shelter
(Hibiscus Children's Center), and to a variety of other organizations, and (3) put the remaining cash into my checking account for spending.

I did all of the mathematical calculations, and even filled out deposit slips. I also wrote checks and balanced my own checkbook.

In 2001, I brought my four-year-old sister Jessie into the business. At the age of six, Jessie was helping to collect the recycling haul, and I taught her the finer points of managing a business, such as filling out a deposit slip and giving a portion back to the environment and others in need.

Gradually, I began spending more and more time on my community service endeavors and allowed Jessie to become a full partner in the recycling programs. Jessie's title is "Vice President of Recycling Services."

With the help of my dad, I have made projections for my business up to my eighteenth birthday. I expect my volume to grow by 10% per year, projecting my recycling efforts to reach 14,820 pounds made up of 296,400 aluminum cans per year. By the year 2009, I projected a recycling total of 140,000 pounds made up of 2,800,000 aluminum cans.

I want other kids and parents to get excited about what I am doing and step forward to lend a hand through participation in additional school and community activities such as environmental fairs and beach clean-ups. I want to encourage everyone to work together to help save the earth's precious resources and "Heal The World" for future generations.

Following in Her Sister's Green Footsteps
Jessica Green
Age 11

How did you get involved in the recycling business?

My older sister, Devon, invited me to become a part of her recycling business when I was five years old, which is how old she was when she started the business. There are two parts of this business and Devon taught me as much about the "giving back" business as the recycling business.

How many clients do you have now?

At first we had over 100 clients, but now we have a lot less because many of them are under new ownership, went out of business, started throwing their cans away, or moved and never contacted us again. Devon has been busy with the "giving back" part of our business as well as college, so she put me in charge of the recycling part. Therefore, I have not attempted to build the number of customers back up because 100 customers were just too many for me to manage on my own. The reduced number of customers has worked out great for me because it keeps us in the recycling business and still allows me time for my volunteer jobs.

What kind of clients do you have, and what do you recycle?

Recycling-wise, there are so many different kinds of organizations that collect cans and other recyclable metals for me. Some of these are: my school, restaurants, banks, offices, auto repair shops, and a lot more.

I recycle for construction businesses. I have recycled for roofers, electricians, plumbers, and general construction businesses. I also recycle brass miss-cut key blanks for the local hardware stores.

We recycle scrap copper and aluminum wires for electricians. We also recycle scrap copper tubing/pipe for plumbers. 'Scrap' means pieces from big rolls of wire or tubing that are left over when the pieces they need for the job have been cut off the roll. We only recycle metals that magnets will not stick to. We use the ABC's of recycling, which are, "A for aluminum, B for brass, C for copper, and S for stainless steel." We definitely recycle more aluminum cans than other metal.

How much money do you make?

When we had 100 customers, we had different week-ly pickup routes and did not pick up from every cus-tomer every week. Reducing the number of customers we serve has allowed us to provide better service over the years. Because of the amount of community ser-vice Devon and I do, and the rising cost of gaso-line, we have recently cut back to a monthly pickup schedule. Therefore what used to be a weekly in-come is now a monthly income. However, Devon has allowed me to have all of the money over the past two years because she's had some other jobs

while she has been in college. The amount of money I get varies greatly based on the market price for scrap metals. For example, aluminum cans were worth about fifty cents a pound last year, but they are only bringing in about thirty cents a pound now. A haul of aluminum cans that would have paid me forty dollars last year is only worth about twenty four dollars now.

Most kids your age don't have a job. What do you do with your money?

Devon taught me everything I know about the busi-ness. She also taught me how to divide my money. I deposit half of the money I earn into my savings ac-count for my college fund, and I am also saving for other important things, like a car. I have a charity en-velope to put ten percent of my spending money into.

Sometimes I put more than ten percent in the charity envelope depending on what else I need money for. During Christmas time, I need more money for buying gifts, so ten percent is the best I can do. What's left, after the charity money is taken out is my spending money for that month.

What kind of volunteer work are you involved with?
    I am the Junior Board Member of the Audubon Society in Stuart, Florida, and I help make decisions for upcoming events, especially the events for children. My fellow board members like to hear what I think children of my age would like. I am also a member of the Humane Society, where I participate in events such as Pet Therapist, when members of the Humane Society go to nursing homes and bring their cat or dog for the people to play with. The Paws to Read program is where members of the Humane Society bring their cat or dog for kids that cannot read on the level of kids their age, so kids can read to the pet. I participate in the Stuart Christmas parade each year with the Pet Therapy volunteers and other various events. I also do fundraising and volunteer for the Hibiscus Children's Center, a local shelter for abused and neglected kids.

What do you like to do, when you're not working?
    In addition to my recycling business and charity involvement, I like to have parties at my house, or sometimes just hang out with one or two friends. I enjoy going to the movies with my whole family. I love to ride on my rip board. My dad, my sister and I have taken tennis lessons. I have a new tennis racket and love to play with my friends as well as Dad and my sister. I also have fun playing basketball with my friends and my teacher at school. Next year, when I'm in the sev-

enth grade, I hope to join the girls' basketball team.

What is your favorite subject at school?

If I had to choose a favorite subject, I guess it would either be Science or English. Besides the fun things I learn in school, there is a science store near my mom's office, and I just love to go there. I have already taken some special classes at this store in Biology, Chemistry, Physics, and Electronics.

What would you like to tell other kids who want to make a difference for their world or their environment?

Thank you for giving me the opportunity to write about "Heal the World" for your book; by sharing our story, other kids will see that "it can be done" by starting small and having a dream for bigger things. Most important, they need to "believe in themselves." We are just average kids like them and look what we have been able to do. My sister has had a special slogan since she was five years old, and I believe it's still true today. "I may be only one person, but I can be one person who makes a difference."

3
Reduce

"Did you know that the most popular vehicle in the world is the bicycle? There are more than a billion bicycles in the world, and less than 500 million cars."

CU Environmental Center

Black Gold
Compost and Composting
By Jake Henty
Age 11
His mother, Brenda Henty owns
My Green Boutique
www.mygreenboutique.com

Hi, my name's Jake and I'm eleven years old. I live in St. Louis, Missouri. I'm going to tell you about compost (black gold), how I got into it, and how to make it.

Compost is nutrient-rich soil that anyone can make, including you. Composting is good for the environment because it uses ordinary stuff like yard and kitchen waste and keeps them out of landfills.

Landfills pollute the earth, so we want to do all we can to reduce them like composting and recycling. I got into composting through a class I took at an advanced learning center. I think we should compost because we have the responsibility of caring for our environment and we can make a difference.

There are four ingredients to compost: air, water, browns (dead leaves, sticks, paper and anything else that is dead and brown) **and greens** (fruits, vegetables, green grass clippings and other yard and kitchen waste). Make sure none of your ingredients have any toxins or oils like mayo or peanut butter.

When you have your ingredients, **make sure you have an equal amount of greens and browns** (maybe a few more greens as they will turn into browns.)

You can buy compost bins online and at most garden stores. I made my own out of two two-liter soda bottles and put kitchen scraps and leaves and whatever else into it. **A good bin should be at least three feet tall, wide and long.** Some bins may be circular or shaped like a trash can, and this is okay.

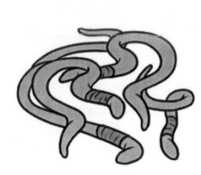

Bugs like worms and pill bugs also help decompose and even flies are okay. Some big composting companies compost meat and other items but for your compost you should probably stay away from meat and dairy products, although eggshells without the yokes would work fine.

Depending on how much compost you plan to make, **the process should take about 6-9 months** (possibly more if you have lots of ingredients). Be sure not to use very much water. A light sprinkle of the hose for 5-10 seconds should do for a couple weeks, but always be sure there is some moisture in your compost. You should stir or mix up your compost once to twice a week (some bins are built to stir—if yours isn't, use a shovel or pitchfork). **Always feel free to add more ingredients but remember to try and keep a balance of browns and greens,** although if there isn't, it's not the end of the world.

You know your compost is right if it doesn't smell like garbage, for one (although it will have an odor).

Two, good compost will give off the tiniest bit of heat. Stick a thermometer into the compost and compare that temperature to the temperature outside. Finally, and most importantly, your compost should be a dark brown or black and have about the same density, if not more compact, than soil.

Remember, this earth is all we have, so go green and keep it clean. Get out there and make a difference. Compost!

Four-Year-Old Composter
I recently decided my four-year-old daughter, Mia is old enough to start doing daily chores and allowed her to pick what she wanted to do. Besides feeding pets and picking up toys she chose to take the items to the compost pile and our vermin composting bin (we have earthworms that eat our vegetable kitchen scraps and in turn make wonderful organic soil for our plants). Claudia McCracken Norton

Greening up Your Power
By Dotty Simmons
Simmon's Naturals
Simmonsnaturals.com

Using alternative energy sources is a broader and less mechanical/technological topic than one might suppose. We all do it. When we **walk to the store** instead of driving, our legs become an alternative energy source. **Closing your curtains** at night will keep your home a little warmer, as opposed to turning the heat up. We can also **wear sweaters around the house**, or add extra blankets on our beds, rather than turning up the thermostat. All of these are important resources for those who want to use other alternative sources of power, such as wind or solar power or alternative fuels. **The key to all alternatives, and petroleum or coal based energy for that matter, is conservation.**

These days, there are more ways to begin to use renewable energy than ever. Whether you live in the city or on a farm, there are ways you can participate. **Many places now have available "green power."** That is, you can choose to buy electricity from a company that generates through wind farms or solar installations.

Biodiesel and/or ethanol fuel pumps are appearing here and there around the nation for people with flex fuel or biodiesel vehicles. **Hybrid gas/electric cars are on the market.** More government incentives are available for putting solar panels on your roof or getting an energy efficient car or appliances. Doing this will create little noticeable change in your life. You still plug in or gas up and drive off.

The changes that really reduce our consumption of the planet's resources take a little more effort and consciousness, **starting with things like turning off lights and appliances you are not using**, insulating and getting rid of drafts and leaks in our homes. This includes unplugging appliances when you are away or overnight, as many have "phantom loads." That is, they still are on a type of "stand-by" mode, using power even after you have turned them off. Make sure all your appliances are energy efficient, **trading in old models for Energy Star models if needed.** Immediately reducing the power you use will do more than anything else in reducing pollution, greenhouse gases, and dependency on foreign oil.

Many alternative energy electric systems are integrated with the existing power grid. That is, you have **solar Photo Voltaic (PV) panels on your roof** and they are wired to put energy into the main power grid from which you buy your usual electricity. **When the sun is shining, your electric meter runs backwards!** You get credit for the power you have put back into the system and that system acts like a giant battery, storing the power so you have electricity at night or in cloudy weather. **People who live off the grid are not connected to the regional power grid or any power company.** The power they produce must be stored too, usually in a bank of large deep cycle batteries.

Our own system has solar PV panels, a micro-hydro system, and a small wind generator. Together they generate power in favorable conditions (sunny, windy, rainy, or all three). **This power is used to charge up the battery bank.** Nothing runs directly off the PV panels or other sources. The energy in the batteries goes through an inverter, which changes it to regular 120 volt household current, so we can plug in appliances and lights the same as in any other home. However, **the storage capacity of our batteries is finite, which makes us very aware of the power we are using.**

Conservation plays a big part in keeping your batteries from getting low unnecessarily. How frugal you are depends on your system and your inclination, but **you soon never leave a light on in an empty room!**

If you want to use alternative power directly without going off the grid, **there are many ways to simply tap the energy of the sun.** One of the easiest changes to make is **solar hot water.** We are all familiar with how hot water comes out of a hose that has been sitting in the sun. Solar hot water systems work on the same principle. There are several variations on this theme—some that heat the water directly, some which work by heating a different fluid and using that to transfer heat to the water in your water heater. Those are called **heat exchange systems**. Check in your local area to find someone who sells or installs these systems. If you cannot use a solar hot water system, **consider changing to an on-demand, or tank-less, hot water heater.** Lots of energy goes into making heat, and keeping a tank of hot water up to temperature all the time is a huge waste. **It will make a noticeable difference in your energy consumption (and power bill) to make this switch.**

Passive solar energy is when you reap heat from the sun without using mechanical or technological means. **Having windows on the southern side of your home is an example.** The list goes on and on. If you want to cut down your use of fossil fuels and green up your power consumption, you have a lot of choices. **But always remember the first step is to use less, mainly by not using power when you do not have to.** Conservation will always be the key in preserving resources and living a greener life.

What about Paper?
By Sara Diamond
Graduate Student
Department of Entomology
University of California, Davis

Do you ever think about how much we use paper? Of course we use paper to write and draw on, but we also use paper in our bathrooms, kitchens, cars, doctors' offices, grocery stores, butchers' shops, etc.

Lampshades, car parts, bags, books, tissues, dishes, cups, plates, wrapping, receipts, cards, toys, insulation, flooring, plant pots, tickets, and even candy wrappers are just some of the things made from paper. And, that's just regular paper—let's not forget that cardboard is paper too—just thicker and rougher and usually unbleached.

So what is paper exactly?

Paper is made from pressed plant fibers—specifically cellulose, which is what plant cell walls are made of. If you ever look at paper under a microscope, you can see all the tiny fibers crisscrossing each other. Smoother paper is made of smaller fibers.

Paper has been around for a long time, although ancient paper was much more difficult to make and was used sparingly. As early as 3500 BC, Egyptians beat papyrus plants into parchment called papyrus, which is where we get our word, paper. Sometime around 100 AD, a Chinese court official named Ts'ai Lun invented paper as we recognize it today. He mixed shredded tree bark, hemp and cloth together with water, beat it into pulp, squeezed out the water, and hung it up like a sheet to dry in the sun. Voila, paper!

Today most paper is made in enormous quantities using a highly mechanized process. No matter who is doing the making, they start with a pulp, generally made of wood—but bark, grass, cotton, or other natural fibers (including elephant dung!) can be used as well. In order to make the pulp, the raw material is shredded into tiny pieces, and mixed with water. This pulp is then refined and cleaned to remove all unwanted compounds from the fibers.

If new materials such as wood or grass are used, the non-cellulose parts of the mixture must be removed. **Lignin is especially important to a tree, but difficult to remove from wood pulp.** Lignin is what allows trees to grow tall, gives wood its hardness, and provides the structural support. Since some trees can live for hundreds and even thousands of years, lignin has to last that long too—so it's very tough and durable. This substance makes up 1/4-1/3 the mass of dry wood. The fastest way to remove lignin from pulp is to use chemicals which produce waste that can pollute air, water and soil. Sometimes paper pulp is also bleached, which causes even more toxic chemicals to be released into the environment. Chlorine-based bleaches are especially polluting.

Recycled paper goes through a similar, although less energy intensive, process. Paper fibers can only be recycled 4-6 times as they get smaller and weaker each time, so every batch of recycled paper pulp has some new pulp added to maintain consistent strength and quality. Recycled paper also has to be washed to remove the ink and other compounds. After the pulp has been refined, cleaned, and sometimes bleached, the mixture is poured onto large screens, pressed into the desired thickness and shape, and allowed to dry. Recycling paper does save trees, but the most important part of recycling paper is conserving water and electricity, and releasing less chemical pollution. **Making paper uses a HUGE amount of water!** For every ton (2,000 lbs) of paper recycled, you save at least 30,000 liters of water (as much water as 157 African elephants would drink in a year, and the amount used by an average American family of 4 for 6 weeks) and as much electricity as an average three-bedroom house would use in a year (3000-4000 kWh).

While we may not be able to give up using paper entirely, **it's easy to use less paper.** And the only way to ensure that forests aren't cut down to make paper is to reduce the demand for it. So, what can you do? Here are some suggestions.

Take a Green Leap!

- Carry a cloth handkerchief so you don't need to use paper tissues
- Use cloth grocery bags or a back pack when shopping
- Use cloth napkins and cleaning rags
- Always write on both sides of the paper in your notebook
- Keep using a notebook until all the pages are full
- Keep paper that has only been used a little bit for taking notes or making lists
- Save and reuse gift wrap, paper bags, cardboard boxes and envelopes
- Ask your parents to buy recycled and unbleached paper products
- Be careful about how much toilet paper you use—a big wad is probably too much
- Make sure you recycle all paper you have used. Depending on where you live, this can include cereal boxes, candy wrappers, magazines, newspapers, envelopes, and lots more
- Does your classroom recycle paper? If not, talk to your teacher about it. You can also ask your teacher to look for other information about recycling in schools at: http://www.paperrecycles.org/school_recycling/index.html
- If you shop at a place with bulk food, try buying it in reusable bags instead of packages that produce trash
- Instead of buying greeting or thank you cards, try and make your own from pulp made from recycled paper scraps or dryer lint. Lots of cool recipes for this can be found on the Internet!

- Try to drink out of metal, glass, or plastic containers that can be recycled or re-used instead of cardboard containers, which have non-recyclable coatings on them.

Disposable Water Bottles:
A Problem for the Earth

By Lynn Hasselberger
President & Founder
Icountformyearth.com
myEarth360.com

• 1.25 million disposable water bottles end up in our landfills EVERY HOUR...in the U.S. alone!
Enough to circle the equator every 5.8 days!
• It takes 3-5 liters of water to make just one l-liter bottle, according to the America Recycling Institute. What a waste, especially when you consider the number of people without any access to clean drinking water!

• It takes 1.5 million barrels of fossil fuels to manufacture and transport bottled water.
Enough to fuel 100,000 cars for one year!
• Disposable water bottles take up to 1,000 years to biodegrade, according to the Container

45

Recycling Institute.

•   25% or more of bottled water is really just tap water in a bottle, sometimes further treated, sometimes not (according to the Natural Resources Defense Council).

•   Chemicals called phthalates, which are known to disrupt testosterone and other hormones, can leach into bottled water over time.

We **can** make a difference, one family, one bottle at a time.

Plastic Bags Contaminate Land and Sea
From Sara Sikes, age 13
Dennard, Arkansas

A study in the 1970s found that all together, ocean-going vessels dumped 8 million pounds of plastic annually. The real reason the world's landfills were not overflowing with plastic was that most grocery bags didn't end up in the landfill. The bags which were dumped into an ocean-fill were being blown around to different parts of our world. They have been seen floating

north of the Arctic Circle and further.

Plastic **grocery bags account for over 10% of the debris** that has washed up on the US coast line. Over time, they break up onto smaller, more toxic particles, setting off fumes. Sadly, this plastic has become part of the food chain for animals. They mistakenly eat it because they think it is food. **The effect on our wildlife is catastrophic and unthinkable.** Birds become terminally entangled and die of starvation in their weakened condition; they are more likely to be devoured by larger animals. Nearly 200 different species of sea life including whales, dolphins, seals, and turtles die due to plastic bags.

There Is a Solution. If we use cloth bags at the grocery store, we can save six plastic bags (or more) per week. That is 24 bags a month, which equals 288 bags a year. That is a savings of 22,176 bags in an average lifetime! If just 1 out of 5 people in each country did this, we would save an outrageous amount over a lifetime.

Ireland made a difference in Europe by taxing plastic bags in 2002. They have reduced plastic bag use by 90%.

The countries of Bangladesh, Israel, Canada, Western India, Botswana, Kenya, Tanzania, South Africa, Taiwan, and Singa-

pore have banned plastic bags.

San Francisco was the first US city to ban plastic bags.

China is saving 37 million barrels of oil each year due to their ban of free plastic bags. If you stop using plastic bags, you will cut down on your country's dependency on foreign oil, protect the lives of innocent wildlife, and make a difference in the fight against pollution.

*U.S. Academy of Science; British Antarctic Survey; Wildlife Fund Report-2005; CNN.com/technology Nov. 16, 2007; BBC News Aug. 20, 2002

Sara prepared this talk for her 4-H group, with the help of a PowerPoint by *Vishal Mody, Physics/Science Teacher, Taft High School, 6530 West Bryn Mawr Avenue, Chicago, IL 6063*

A side note from Sara's mom: "[This report] made me sad about the waste. It inspired Sara to get on the bandwagon to stop using plastic bags. I'm excited about the change it brought about. We now have everyone in our 4H group using only cloth bags at the store. We even take a cloth bag into stores like Dollar General and Family Dollar, anywhere they use plastic bags." Jackie Sikes

Why Are Families Concerned about Chinese Products?
By Jill A. Vanderwood
What's It Like, Living Green?

Asbestos and lead are showing up in products

intended for children.

Asbestos: With Chinese imports to the US and around the world, we are taking the brunt of lax Chinese environmental practices. In 2007, CBS contracted a Chinese company to make a child's CSI Fingerprint Examination Kit. **High levels of asbestos were found in this product,** as well as in two brands of children's molding clay. Asbestos also showed up in powdered cleanser, roof sealers, duct tapes, window glazing, spackling paste and small appliances, according to the Asbestos Disease Awareness Organization. Seattle Pi.com

Asbestos was thought to be a miracle product. Researchers admit, "asbestos is a truly wondrous material. In a technological world it is a manufacturer's dream." It's stronger than steel, but still flexible, it's fire resistant, chemical resistant and great for insulation and acoustics. The main problem is that it kills people. It is one material that can save your life while making you sick. Asbestos causes a number of illnesses, including a lung cancer called Mesothelioma.
http://www.m3associates.co.uk/Images/What_is_asbestos.pdf

Asbestos has been banned in 40 countries. It is still used in the US. It was not until 1973 that work places began reducing asbestos exposure. Since asbestos is considered more hazardous to remove than to leave undisturbed, it is still found in older homes and schools. Mesothelioma-lung-cancer.org

China is the largest miner of asbestos, which is an ore, and their asbestos use continues to rise with no thought of the health consequences to the mostly poor, uneducated and uninsured Chinese workers.
*from the World Asbestos Report. A website from the Mainland of China-- Alibaba.com lists 2,959 Products made from Asbestos.

Lead Paint was banned in the US in 1977, according to the Consumer Product Safety Commission. Since then, **lead has been treated as a hazardous waste,** and removed from older buildings by crews with protective suits and face masks.

When lead paint began showing up on dinnerware and children's toys, these products were traced back to Chinese manufacturers.

Trusted toy companies, which produced toys from popular TV programs for very young children, have had numerous **toys recalled due to lead paint.** Children are likely to chew on a toy and swallow the paint. Metal jewelry with the names of popular preteen stars has also been recalled, due to the lead content.

Lead poisoning can cause learning disabilities, behavioral problems, and, at very high levels, seizures, coma, and even death.
http://www.koat.com/news/4469339/detail.htm and Healthytoy.org

After February 2009, **products** available in the US which are intended to be used by children under twelve **will be tested for lead, phthalates, and cadmium.** Products containing these products at levels above the allowable limits will be considered banned hazardous materials.

To be sure whether a toy is safe, you can **do a search on healthytoy.org.** You may sign up for the newsletter, announcing results of additional testing.

China is also known to use pesticides, long banned by the US, Canada, Europe and other countries. Much of the Chinese produce is exported.

The **top ten most-polluted cities** in the world are all located in China. Efforts are now being made to take care of their inferior sanitation practices.

China is not known for fair-trade practices; they are without regard to the treatment or fair pay for their workers.

Chinalaborwatch.org; beyond pesticides.org; motherjones.com; The Christian Science Monitor

If China continues to pollute the water and air, it also affects people all over the world. Do we really want to continue to purchase inferior products from an environmentally unaware country?

Energy Saving Tips
from Carrol Wolverton
Living Cheap and Loving It:
tomatoes in the flower garden

Energystar.com makes several excellent recommendations:
•   They promote the use of **CFLs**, which are the compact fluorescent light bulbs. **These bulbs consume 75% less energy** and last up to ten times longer than regular light bulbs. I have been purchasing them gradually as I've seen them on sale and have replaced

Take a
Green
Leap!

our most frequently used bulbs. Older bulbs remain in rarely used locations, such as in the attic and the back of closets.

• **Set your water heater to 120** degrees or less. Remember, there are top and bottom settings. Turn off the electricity before doing this. Your water heater carries a 220-volt punch. If you need to replace a water heater, check with the electric company. Ours is offering a discount on the electric bill if you use a certain energy-efficient model.

• **Keep** heat and air flow **registers clean** and uncovered by drapes or furniture so the flow is not restricted. It's rather silly to have insulated, cost-saving drapes if they cover a register and direct the heat straight up and against the window.

• **Seal air leaks** with caulk. Old caulk cracks and falls out. I've found re-caulking helps with bug reduction also.

• **Shut down** the computer after use. Then turn off the power strip at the switch.

• The **microwave can save 80%** of your cooking energy use.

• **When heating a pan** on the stove, use the right size burner. If you put a six-inch pan on an eight-inch burner, 40% of the energy is wasted, according to the Energy Star folks.

How Can You Reduce Greenhouse Gases?
By Jill A. Vanderwood
What's it Like, Living Green?

Greenhouse gases are caused by the use of carbon dioxide. Sometimes our use of carbon is called our **carbon footprint.**

Greenhouse gases form an invisible cloud that keeps the warm air down and the cold air up. These gases are leading to another problem for the earth, called **global warming.**

When we use electricity, we are contributing to greenhouse emissions. Most electricity comes from power plants. Normally, **power plants use coal and oil to make electricity.** Burning coal and oil produces greenhouse gases.

You are helping to send greenhouse gas into the air by...

    Watching TV
    Playing video games
    Listening to the radio
    Blow drying your hair
    Using a car for transportation
    Turning on a light
    Using the microwave

Factories produce greenhouse gases, but even the trash that goes to the landfill and the animals that are raised for food produce a gas called **methane**—which **is also a greenhouse gas**.

Global Warming is created by greenhouse gases. Some warming is good. By having warmer weather, some areas will have a climate to produce more of their own food.

Too much warming can cause glaciers to melt, which also causes the sea to expand. This rapid change can cause disasters, like flooding. These climate changes can force both animals and humans to lose their homes. Too much flooding can also affect the food and clean water supply.

Too many warm days can also cause health problems and the possibility of water shortages. Too much rain or not enough rain will cause an imbalance in nature and animal habitats.

Take a Green Leap!

What Can We Do to Cut Down on Greenhouse Gases?
- **Turn off the lights, TV and computer when you aren't using them**
- **Walk, ride your bike or take the bus whenever you can**
- **Let other people know about climate change and greenhouse gases**
- **Plant trees—trees absorb carbon dioxide**
- **Recycle cans, plastic and newspapers to save trash from the landfill and save energy used to produce these products**
- **Buy recycled or recyclable products**

Information from the EPA Global Warming Kids Site

4
Reuse

"In my life I have tried to do the best I could to walk softly on this mother earth and have incorporated many choices and methods to do what I feel to be best."
Jeanette Ammon-single mother from Albany, Ohio

The Keeper
Author Unknown

I grew up in the 40s/50s with practical parents.

A mother, God love her, who washed aluminum foil after she cooked in it, then reused it. She was the original recycle queen, before they had a name for it.

A father who was happier getting old shoes fixed than buying new ones.

Their marriage was good, their dreams focused.

Their best friends lived barely a wave away. I can see them now, Dad in trousers, T-shirt and a hat and Mom in a house dress, lawn mower in one hand, and dish towel in the other.

It was the time for fixing things. A curtain rod, the kitchen radio, screen door, oven door, the hem in a dress. Things we keep.

It was a way of life, and sometimes it made me crazy. All that re-fixing, eating, renewing... I wanted just once to be wasteful.

Waste meant affluence. Throwing things away meant you knew there'd always be more.

But then my mother died, and on that clear summer's

night, in the warmth of the hospital room, I was struck with the pain of learning that sometimes there isn't any more. Sometimes, what we care about most gets all used up and goes away…never to return.

So…while we have it…it's best we love it…and care for it…and fix it when it's broken…and heal it when it's sick.

This is true for marriage…..and old cars…and children with bad report cards…and dogs with bad hips…and aging parents…and grandparents.

We keep them because they are worth it, because we are worth it. Some things we keep.

Like best friends who moved away or classmates we grew up with. There are just some things that make life important.

WASTE
by Carrol Wolverton
Living Cheap and Loving It: tomatoes in the flower garden

So many times I buy things other people just don't want to mess with.

Quality shirts with a missing button often have an extra button sewn into a seam. So fix the thing. At a resale shop, I purchased a new jeans skirt that had part of the zipper seam pulled apart so the zipper puckered. Less than a minute of effort on my twenty-year-old sewing machine repaired it. A wrought-iron fireplace screen with a broken hinge was fixed with a small amount of JB Weld. The new $200 heavy-duty screen door on my back porch came from a garage sale for $10.

Freecycle
By Linda Stein
Owner of Zosimos Botanicals LLC
Gaithersburg, MD
www.zosimosbotanicals.com

I am the mother of two children, a three-year-old girl named Hannah and a five-year-old boy named Jacob. **When we need something, we try to get it on Freecycle before thinking of buying it new.**

Freecycle is an organization with groups around the world. Individuals **post items to give away.** Nothing can be sold or bartered. The purpose of Freecycle is to reuse items that still have a useful life, rather than throwing them in the trash, where they will end up in a landfill. Reusing items rather than making new ones saves money and energy.

The first item our family obtained from Freecycle was a computer for our son. A man who works in the IT department of his office posted a computer to give away. I drove to his house, and he even loaded it into the back of the van for me.

Joining Freecycle is simple. The website is freecycle.org. There is a locator to find the group closest to your home. This is important, because once an item has been set aside for you, it must be picked up from the person giving it away. Freecyclers do not mail items to each other. It is done on a very local, community-based level.

The first thing we gave away on Freecycle was a pair of rose bushes. When my son Jacob started to walk, it was a big worry that he would hurt himself on the rose thorns. A lovely woman came and dug them up to replant in her yard. Everyone we have met on Freecycle is very happy to receive their items, even if they have to put some effort into taking them home!

Plants that grow from bulbs multiply and need to be thinned out. We have obtained beautiful orange Daylilies for our yard when people gave away the extra bulbs they dug up.

Typical things that are posted in our Freecycle network are children's clothing, furniture, computers, kitchen items and toys. Many people move and don't want to take everything with them to the new house. Babies outgrow clothing very quickly, and sometimes clothing is not worn at all. Often family members give new parents gifts and the babies simply don't have a chance to wear everything before growing out of the size, or won't fit into winter clothes until it is summer.

My kids frequently go with me to pick up things which are being given away by Freecyclers. **Jacob and Han-**

nah think clothes and toys come from people's houses! We have received a train table, doll house, lots of Barbie dolls with clothes, a scooter for Hannah, a toy chest and more.

Here is how the system works. A person giving an item away posts it on the Freecycle list. Other members of the list see the post. **If you want the item, you have to respond immediately with a proposed day and time to pick it up.**

The person giving the item away will provide the address or directions. Most of the time, small items are left outside the front door in a plastic bag with the intended pickup person's name on it. It is not unusual for several bags, with different names, to be waiting for pickup.

The biggest problem is caused by people not showing up to pick up items as arranged. This discourages the givers, especially if they are new to Freecycle. If I am giving things away, I keep emails from several responders just in case the first person doesn't show up. Then I can tell the next person in line to come without having to re-post the item. After participating for awhile, the people in the network start becoming familiar.

Once, a plea was posted for a family whose house had burned down. The children had lost all of their toys in the fire. I told my kids that a little boy, slightly younger than my son, had no toys. I asked my children to find toys in the playroom to give to the little boy. My children selflessly filled a large white garbage bag with toys. The day the bag was picked up, my son was so happy to see that the little boy got the toys. He beamed with happiness.

I run a green cosmetics business out of our home. Being green means we reduce, reuse and recycle as much as we can.

We reuse all of the packing material from packages delivered to our studio to cushion the outgoing make-up. **The entire workshop is outfitted with items from Freecycle.**

Freecyclers have provided the tables, bookcases, microwave, chairs, refrigerator, corkboard, pegboard, white board, the baby food and mason jars we use for storage, the clock and mirror.

People who come to the studio and learn how it was furnished are amazed.

The best resource Freecycle offers are the participants.

Since our family began participating in Freecycle, we have heard many heartwarming stories, learned of the amazing generosity in our community and made sure useful things have homes where they are fully appreciated rather than thrown away.

How to Reuse Household Items
from Emily Sikes, age 15
From Arkansas

We do a lot of crafts out of things around the house. We reduce the amount of trash we make and we recycle everything we can.

• **Old Christmas Cards** can be used to make **ornaments**. To make ornaments: cut two cards into

any shape. Glue them front to back. Punch a hole in the top and hang them with some yarn or string.

• **Toilet paper rolls** can be made into **bird feeders or candy rolls** for nursing homes. To make toilet paper roll bird feeders: simply cover the roll with peanut butter, and then coat it in bird seed. Thread some string or yarn through it and hang your feeder from a tree. For candy rolls: take toilet paper rolls and fill them with hard candies, then wrap them with tissue paper, tying both ends with ribbon—like a present.

• **Telephone books** can be made into **Christmas angels**. First, fold down the top of each page until it reaches the center of the book. Depending on the size of the book, you may need to use two telephone books of the same size. This is the body of the angel. Next, you need to hot glue the back and fronts of both books together. Then, spray paint the body with paint of any color. Add a round Styrofoam head to the top. Draw a face or use googly eyes, or buttons for the eyes. Use a glitter chenille wire for a halo and yarn or fake fur for the hair.

• You can **use scraps of paper** to make a **paper chain** for a garland around your tree or for decorations for birthday parties.

• You can use **different types and sizes of boxes** to make **doll furniture**. One year my sister and I made a whole house full of furniture for my nieces to use with their Barbie dolls. My favorite was the bath tub made with a rectangular Kleenex box. We put batting inside to make it look like a tub full of bubbles.

•   **Large and small boxes can be used as building blocks and forts**. Your children can even use boxes from cereal, cake mixes or Kleenex to play 'store' with. When they are crushed and you can't use them anymore, recycle them at a recycling center. Our center will take cardboard wet or dry.

•   **Paper egg cartons can be used as fire starters.** Take a paper egg carton and fill it with lint from your dryer. This can be used to start a fire in your fireplace or at a campfire.

•   **Glass bottles and jars** make great **flower vases or candle holders**. You can take small twigs and hot glue them to the side of a jar for a pretty, "natural" vase. You can make new candles in jars by melting wax, adding your favorite scent and a new wick. Or, you can take old candles and re-melt them to make new candles.

•   **With a glass jar and a lid** you can make a **cinnamon and sugar shaker**. Simply take a jar lid and hammer holes in the top with a nail. Next, fill the jar with cinnamon and sugar, attach the lid and you have a cinnamon and sugar shaker.

•   **You can use a jar with a lid to make gravy.** My mom uses a plain old jar to make lump-free gravy. First, she pours in a small amount of milk. Then she adds flour and shakes it well. When it's free of lumps, she slowly stirs this mixture into pan drippings. You can add more as needed. *The shaking gets rid of the lumps that sometimes form if flour is added right to the drippings.

•   **Jars with lids or tubs with lids can be used as banks.** Cut a slit in the plastic tub lid or jar lid, large enough for coins. It is fun to paint and decorate the jars or tubs with stickers, lace or jewels. Now you are ready to start saving money.

• **Plastic tubs can be used as planters.** Use plastic tubs such as yogurt or butter containers to make planters. This is a great way to get seeds started then transfer them to your garden.

• **Plastic bags can be used as packing material** when mailing packages. There are books out there that show you how to make placemats, rugs etc. out of plastic bags like you get from Wal-Mart.

• **Two-liter soda pop bottles make good bird feeders.** Drill two holes at bottom of the bottle, directly across from each other. Make one hole slightly larger than the other one. Stick a large wooden spoon into the holes, and then fill the bottle, from the top, with bird seed. Be sure to stick the bowl of the spoon into the hole that is slightly larger than the other one, so bird-

seed will spill out onto the spoon. Drill two holes at the neck of the bottle and run a string through them for hanging. The birds will sit on the spoon and peck at the holes for the bird-seed.

• **Plastic juice bottles or plastic soda bottles** can be used as **bowling pins or a bean bag toss**. There are all kinds of games you can play with plastic bottles. We always recycle our aluminum cans, but you could use cans in the same way.

• **Old T-shirts make good pillows.** Turn your old T-shirts inside out, and sew the neck, across the top of the sleeves, and one third of the bottom of the shirt.

Turn the shirt right side out, and stuff with fiber fill. Finish sewing the bottom of the shirt by hand. You have a very soft pillow with personality to decorate your room.

• **Socks make great puppets, snowmen or dolls.** *Note: this works better with a tube sock that doesn't have a heel. To make a snowman or doll, stuff your sock with batting. Use yarn to tie off the head, part way down the opening of the sock. If you are making a snowman, tie off the sock in two different places to help form the head, tummy and bottom. Tie the sock one to two inches from the opening, where you filled the sock, then fold the top down over the head of the doll or the snowman to look like a cap. Now you are ready to add a face with buttons or markers. If you are making a snowman, add additional buttons down the front.

• **With reusable clothing and toys, you can have a free kid swap yard sale.** Everyone will bring things to the swap. Each kid can swap out their items for 'new' items for free. If you bring five things, you get to take five things home. My sister and I are home-schooled, and we do a similar thing with our old school books. When we have completed a book, we offer it to someone else who needs it.

• **Tin cans can be made into pencil holders.**

• **Old crayons can be melted to make candles,** or added to melted wax to make your candle the color you like.

Driving Green:
My Biodiesel Car
By Jeanette Ammon
Single mother of two
Albany, Ohio

In my life I have tried to do the best I could to walk softly on this mother earth and have incorporated many choices and methods to do what I feel to be best.

I first heard friends at a potluck dinner talking about cars running on grease. I still had this idea in mind when I read an article in the local newspaper about a young man who does grease conversions for cars. After talking to several friends, **I learned that you could actually run converted grease in a relatively unaltered diesel car** and this sold me on the concept. First I spoke with the local bio-fuel producer to be certain I could get the fuel as I needed it.

Next, I purchased my 1982 diesel Mercedes. **As far as I know, diesels are the only vehicles that can run on grease.**

My Mercedes was retrofitted with seals that are of a more durable Vicon rubber, so the grease won't eat through the seals, causing them to leak.

I buy my biodiesel fuel from an acquaintance, who does a grease conversion—rather than a car conversion. He blends methanol with used and filtered cooking grease from restaurants to remove impurities and glycerin so it can run directly into the normal fuel tank of a vehicle.

At first he was able to get the grease from restaurants for free, but as the demand has increased in our area, now he must pay for it. In addition to individuals who buy the fuel for personal use, he sells converted grease for use in farm equipment and larger trucks.

I have been driving my biodiesel car for over a year and I'm happy with the performance of the grease. Although it was recommended to me to blend this fuel with regular diesel, during cold weather last winter, I found the car started more smoothly and rapidly with the converted grease alone.

If I'm planning to take a long trip, **I try to carry extra fuel in five gallon containers in the trunk of my car.** The fumes from regular diesel make me feel nauseated and it's more expensive at the pump and for the environment. **My fuel burns cleaner** and smells like French fries, Chinese food or other random foods, depending what was cooked in the grease.

I have been fortunate to have my fuel delivered at **a minimum of .25 cents cheaper than the going rate at the stations,** which has been a bit tricky with the price fluctuations, but it suits me fine. My fuel comes in 55-gallon drums, so I purchased a hand-powered fuel pump to deliver it to my car. **My car has been fueled with used grease ever since I purchased it one year ago, and it gets around 30 mpg.** It is an older car so I am not sure if this is the best it has gotten over the years, when it was running on diesel.

Now that my daughter is sixteen, she has learned to drive with my biodiesel car. We share the car and it's the only car she has ever driven.

Driving this car that reduces emissions, waste and reuses fuel has been a choice that has proven worthy. I do not drive more since using this car. I still try to combine trips, carpool and drive less, whenever possible.

Ethan's Green Choices
By Lynn Hasselberger
IcountformyEarth.com
Myearth360.com

In 2006, when my son, Ethan, started soccer and tee ball, I witnessed the bottled water phenomenon like never before.

When we would carpool with other families, parents had cases of bottled water to dole out from the back of SUVs before, during and after sports practice and games. Other parents had garage refrigerators stocked full of bottled water and Gatorade, as if their children were training for a triathlon.

I was already concerned about the environment and the plight of the polar bear, but it was my son who inspired me to take action.

When Ethan entered first grade, we were instructed by the school to pack water for our children daily. **Never a fan of bottled water, I packed a reusable bottle for my son.** It took no time for my son to complain about being the only one who doesn't pack a plastic bottle (disposable water bottle). I explained to him how wasteful and costly bottled water was, and the negative impact it had on the environment. And he never looked back!

One day, Ethan found bottled water (one lonely half-full bottle that my husband, Craig, had somehow purchased under the radar) in our refrigerator and just about hit the roof. "Mom! What is that doing in our refrigerator?" Another day, Ethan tattled on Craig for having an empty bottle in his car's cup holder. He began reminding my husband to turn off the lights and hoof it to the next errand if it was within walking distance. **Ethan took great pride in alerting us (yes, even me... I'm not 100% perfect, yet) of our own environmental missteps.** One day it hit me. Wouldn't all children, if so inspired, serve as daily environmental champions within their homes?

I custom designed reusable water bottles and developed I Count for myEARTH, an environmental awareness campaign geared toward elementary school children, which launched in January 2008 at Ethan's school. Neighbors and friends started asking my advice about other things and myEARTH360.com was born to support my passion for helping families transition to an earth-friendlier lifestyle.

When I go out with Ethan and talk to people on the streets, he (now seven and a half) speaks up about bottled water, why we say no to plastic bags and blurts out the website address and phone number!

Recently, a cashier asked him if he'd like a bag for one pack of gum and Ethan laughed and said, "Of course not." He then turned to me, shrugging and asked, "Mom, why'd he ask me that?" He's been on play dates and forgotten his reusable water bottle and my friends admonish me about his refusal to accept bottled water, even when thirsty and nothing else is available on a 90 degree day at the park (I am not kidding). He thinks twice about how to spend his money at Target, although I'm planning an intervention for his and my husband's Lego addiction. I have to tell him not to point at people who carry bottled water or don't bring their reusable shopping bag. I tell him we're not here to judge, we are here to inspire others, to help them transition to an earth-friendlier lifestyle and understand why that is good for the earth and the health and well-being of generations to come.

Reuse Tips From-
Jill A. Vanderwood
What's it Like, Living Green?

• When planning a **backyard barbeque,** I invited guests to bring a potluck dish and their own reusable utensils, plates and cups. This cut down on the waste of plastic and paper products.

• Are you planning a **picnic at the park?** Bring along your own reusable dishes and utensils. Have you seen the overflowing trash cans at the park?

•   Do you **pack lunches** for your family for work or school? There is no need to buy paper lunch bags or sandwich bags. We use lunch boxes and reusable sandwich-sized containers.

•   Do you **pack chips or cookies** for lunches? Try using small reusable containers, which fit right into a lunch box.

•   What about plastic utensils? Sam's Club® or Costco® carry **stainless steel utensils** in restaurant packs of spoons, forks or knives at a reasonable price. These won't match your regular utensils, but they come in handy for yogurt or dessert, and they won't cause waste in a landfill.

•   Are you trying to **cut back on the use of paper towels**? K-mart® sells bulk packages of thin wash-cloths. These are very handy for quick clean-ups and they can also work well in a lunch box, as a napkin.

•   When I started carrying **a reusable water bottle** to work, I soon noticed that everyone else began carrying one as well.

•   If you are like me, **it's hard to remember to bring the cloth bags into the grocery store**, even though they are in my car. I've found something that helps. If I get up to the checkout without the bags, I ask the cashier to load my groceries back into the

cart, without bags. I then take the food to my car and pack the items into my own bags. Soon, to avoid embarrassment, you will remember your bags.

•   **Stores in my area offer a five-cent credit** for any reusable grocery bags you use. They also give

me that same credit when I refuse a bag.

•	Be sure to watch when someone is bagging your food. The **baggers are so fast**, they may have all of your groceries bagged before you hand them your reusable bags.

•	**Don't be afraid to make a change.** Your example will help others to take a green leap.

5
Responsible for Our Earth

"All of us make choices every single day that have an environmental impact. Some choices keep energy and resource use low, while other choices have a high environmental cost."
Wynne Coplea—Environmental Educator

The World
By Sara Sikes-age 13

Let's save the world together,
before it dies,
and we'd better strike hard the very first time.

We need to recycle,
and help the world,
stop pollution.

If it's going to end now,
we'd better hop to it,
and find a solution.

Stop using so much water,
turn off all the lights.
Don't use plastic bags,
let's make this thing right.

We need to recycle and recycle fast,
So we can live in a world without toxic gas.

Come on, let's work together
to make everything better.

We want our grandchildren to look back and see
that we saved the future and made history.

What Does It Mean
To Be Green at a Park?
By Wynne Coplea-Environmental Educator

Edwin Watts Southwind Park and Erin's Pavilion in Springfield, Illinois are specially **designed to be used by people of all abilities**. This means that even if someone is in a wheelchair, is blind or deaf, or has developmental disabilities, they can still use and enjoy Southwind Park. The sidewalks are color-coded for sighted people and have special grooves so sight-impaired people with canes can tell which way they should go. The playground, gazebo and fishing piers on the lake are designed to make it easy for anyone to walk or roll up.

The restrooms and picnic shelters are also easily accessible, and are **lit by solar power, while a turbine generates electricity from the wind.** Kids will enjoy finding the fossils embedded in the bottom of the babbling brook. **How about a fully accessible tree house?** Southwind Park's tree house is specially designed so that even wheelchairs can go up into it.

There are a **variety of different gardens** in Southwind Park, including a Fragrance Garden featuring plants and flowers chosen for their smell, and a Sensory Garden full of plants and flowers with a variety of textures, meant to be touched.

Springfield Park District

The entire park and even the parking lots feature beautiful plants and flowers that were chosen because

they are native to Illinois and will have an easier time growing and blooming here. It also means they take less water to grow, and water conservation is important to Southwind Park. Native plants bloom and grow in little concrete islands in the parking lot called "bioswales," which are designed to absorb rainwater and filter through the native plants before it goes into the storm sewer. This reduces any oils or pollutants that would have gone directly into our water supply.

Erin's Pavilion is named for Erin Elzea, a special young woman from Springfield. Erin had many disabilities that made it hard for her to learn and play like other children. In spite of this, she lived a full and active life and attended school in Springfield. When Erin passed away, her family decided that helping to build Erin's Pavilion and the Southwind Park would be a great tribute to Erin, so families would have a place that was easy for them to play and explore together.

Erin's Pavilion has been built using recycled materials that came mostly from within a 500-mile radius of Springfield. The building was carefully planned and designed to be energy efficient, to conserve water, and to use recycled products. All of these eco-friendly aspects of Erin's Pavilion and Southwind Park are part of the requirements needed for qualifying for a LEED platinum rating. The US Green Building Council has created a point system called LEED for Leadership in Energy Efficient Design, with different rating levels awarded to sites based on their environmental features.

The goal of a LEED platinum rating meant the **designers of Erin's Pavilion had to work harder to locate building materials made from recycled products.** For example, the countertops in the pavilion are made of a material called PaperStone, which is made from crushed stone and used paper. The doors are made with an interior core of wheat straw, and an exterior of bamboo. Unlike other materials that may take years to grow, **bamboo can sometimes grow at a rate of 20 feet per day! We call this a rapidly renewable material.**

The carpet is made from recycled products; all of the paint inside the building is made from materials that have low toxins, making it a healthier environment. Throughout the building, many **windows are placed to capture sunlight so electric lighting is not needed.** On the roof of Erin's Pavilion are solar photovoltaic panels which collect and provide power from the sun. Also, the roof is angled so rain filters into pipes underground that go to the lake. The **lake water is used to water the grass** on the great lawn and help heat **and cool the pavilion**, using a hydro-geothermal system. This means large pipes are sunk deeply into the ground to pull heat from the earth's core. Other pipes run in a loop under the lake and use the temperature of the lake's water to heat or cool these pipes, depending on the weather.

If you decide to visit Southwind Park and Erin's Pavilion, you may get to take a tour by riding on a specially designed accessible tram. Or, if you find there is no guide available to take you on a tour, you can check out a hand-held computer unit to take you on a guided "virtual" tour. The Ranger is about the size of an electronic game controller, and is encoded with Global Positioning System technology. The GPS system guides visitors on a tour around the park's 2.5 mile trail, and features short videos telling interesting stories about the park and pavilion. **Trivia questions will test your knowledge of environmental facts** and what you know about Southwind Park and Erin's Pavilion.

As you enter Erin's Pavilion, you can use our electronic guestbook to sign in and tell where you are from. You can also look at a map showing where other visitors to the park have come from and access information about special events and programs. **You can view the visual display of information about the pavilion's energy use,** energy generated from wind and solar units, and water usage. Displaying and tracking this kind of information can help us manage our resources and always be conscious of our environmental impact.

All of us make choices every single day that have an environmental impact. Some choices keep energy and resource use low, while other choices have a high environmental cost. **When we make choices that purposefully keep use of resources to a minimum, and try to save resources for future generations to use, this is called being sustainable.** Southwind Park and Erin's Pavilion are models for other parks and public buildings by being both accessible for all people, and environmentally sustainable.

Chocolate—a Yummy Treat?
By Jill A. Vanderwood
What's It Like, Living Green?

In the US, you can find Halloween candy in stores as early as July. Just walking by the display makes my mouth water. The store owners hope that by putting candy out early, you will buy several bags, open the candy and eat it, having to buy more before trick-or-treaters come on October 31st .

Before Halloween, you will find a pleasing array of Christmas chocolates. Before Christmas arrives, those have been replaced by heart-shaped boxes of Valentine candy. Then there are the Easter assortments of malted milk chocolate eggs, chocolate-covered marshmallow eggs, and the list goes on.

We all have our favorite chocolate treats and we probably prefer one brand over another.

But did you ever stop to think that 43 percent of the world's cocoa beans are grown in West Africa, where 284,000 children work on cocoa farms under abusive labor conditions?

Although the chocolate industry brings in $13 billion, those who produce chocolate are not well paid. Cocoa growers in West Africa average between $30 and $110 per household member per year. **Many cocoa farmers use children as laborers** and force them to work long hours under terrible working conditions, with little or no pay.

Did you know that **many countries are cutting down rainforests to grow more cocoa?** For centuries, ca-

cao trees have been grown slowly in the shade and protection of the rainforest. With the desire to grow more cocoa at a faster rate, many farmers are cutting down the rainforests, leaving animals without a home. **Not only are animals displaced, but clearcutting rainforests contributes to global warming.**

By growing the cocoa beans in full sunlight, they can grow faster, producing more chocolate. **The cocoa is more susceptible to disease, insects and the sun.** The farmers are using more fertilizers and stronger pesticides to grow cocoa in full sunlight. The pesticides, long banned from other parts of the world, including the US and Europe, are killing birds, including the bald eagle and the peregrine falcon. Pesticides end up in the air, ground water, and even in the chocolate.
*The UK Pesticide Action Network found residue from lindane in all 20 chocolate bars tested in 1998.

Information comes from: **Solvie Karlstr for the National Geographic Green Guide to Go October 22, 2008**

Hershey has been using organic chocolate since 2006. Now along with other chocolate companies, such as Cadbury and Mars, they are uniting with the World Cocoa Foundation (WCF) to encourage sustainable cocoa production in West Africa. This program, funded by the US Agency for International Development (USAID) and the chocolate companies, aims to help 150,000 farmers and their families over the next five years. The Foundation supports cocoa-growing families by improving working conditions and ensuring better production methods and increased productivity.
Confectionarynews.com

When buying chocolate, look for the words **Fair Trade** products—which means fair wages and fair working conditions; **Rainforest Alliance**—which means the beans were grown in at least 40% shade, protecting wildlife; and **Organic**—which means that pesticides and fertilizers were not used to grow the cocoa beans.

Many products contain chocolate, even when it is not the main ingredient. Ben and Jerry's carries Fair Trade certified chocolate and vanilla ice cream, and Green and Black's has organic chocolate ice cream, as well as chocolate bars. Sunspire carries organic, Fair Trade, chocolate baking chips. www.worldpantry.com

Creating a Backyard Wildlife Preserve
By Claudia McCracken Norton
Crabtree, North Carolina

I first noticed my daughter Mia's environmental awareness when we were picking up trash alongside our road. I heard her singing "Clean up, clean up, people everywhere. Clean up, clean up, everybody do your share." I had no idea where she had heard such a song and assumed it was daycare (she was almost three at the time) but later I heard a similar song on an episode of "Dora the Explorer." **Mia is also a fan of the Nickelodeon environmental initiative "The Big Green Help"** and constantly asks how she can help. When she does something like turning off the water while brushing teeth (or remind her dad to do so as well) she always says it's because she's "part of the Big Green Help." Recently while reading a book from the library, we stumbled upon the organization called Kids F.A.C.E. (Kids for a Clean Environment) and it was started by kids for kids who want to try and make a difference. I wasn't sure that Mia, who is now four years old, was old enough to join but they seemed eager to have such a young member. Mia was very proud of her certificate of membership and fully understands what type of things she can do to be an active member. **I have a feeling that when she starts kindergarten next year she will try to recruit new members to the cause.**

One of the things we have done is to create a backyard wildlife habitat. It's a simple thing in which the entire family can participate and enjoy.

The National Wildlife Federation has a program where they will certify your habitat after you complete an application (along with a small processing fee which in turn funds their wonderful programs) where you list features of your habitat and they confirm you have the elements necessary to sustain wildlife in your yard. **Although we live in a rural area with a large amount of property the concept can be applied to a much smaller yard, as long as you supply wildlife with the necessary elements.** According to the National Wildlife Federation there are **four basic elements you need: water, food, shelter/cover and a place to raise young.** I will tell a little bit about how we accomplished each of these in our yard.

FOOD: Providing food was easy, since **we already had multiple bird feeders in place around our yard.** We have suet feeders, several types of bird feeders that dispense various types of seeds for different bird species (sunflower/peanut and fruit mix for some birds,

thistle for finch, chickadee and small birds as well as a mealworm feeder for insect eaters like bluebirds). **We added a squirrel feeding station** (if you have lots of squirrels, this is a plus as they leave the bird feeders alone), to draw them out of the woods behind our home so we could see them. We have hummingbird feeders in the summer. **We also planted flowers with wildlife in mind.** We have cosmos (*cosmos bipinnatus*), bee balm (*monarda*), butterfly weed (*asclepiadaceae*), perennial verbena, asters, butterfly bush (*buddleia*) and trumpet vine (*incarvillea*); all of which provide food for birds, bees or butterflies.

Water: We put up a **bird bath** in our yard. We also placed several plastic flower pot drain dishes at various locations around the property to serve as **drinking or bathing stations** for other animals. We have some with rocks in them so insects such as  bees and butterflies can safely drink without drowning. These critters seem to prefer more stagnant water, so as long as mosquitoes aren't an issue, it's relatively maintenance free, with the exception of replacing water as it is used. This past summer **we added a small pond with a pump and a fountain** which was very inexpensive to install and maintain. We provided some fish and plants, but it would be a good source of water without the decorations also. **This water feature is a magnet for frogs, and various birds** visit that had never bothered with our other water sources. **Mia loves to feed the fish and watch the frogs** come out each night during the summer. That leads to the next element: shelter.

Shelter: The rocks surrounding the pond do a good job of providing a cool, moist and protected environment for frogs. **We also have numerous "frog and toad huts"** around our yard. We made many ourselves by repurposing old clay flower pots that had chips on the rims. We made the chipped areas big enough to serve as openings in which toads could enter (I sanded the surfaces to insure that no creature would get

scratched by the clay shards). Mia and I had fun painting the outside of the pots. We then placed them open side down on the ground, creating instant toad abodes. **Mia loves to look under them to see if they are inhabited by amphibian guests** (most were, at some point during  the summer). Since we do live in a rural area bordering a forest, we have established brush piles near the edges of our property as additional shelter for wildlife. We installed a **ladybug house** in my tiny rose garden. The ladybugs have a nice shelter, and they eat the aphids that feast on my roses. We also put up **butterfly houses** and have had a few visitors to them. **We keep honeybees on our property,** and decided to help out our native pollinators as well, since they are all facing rapidly decreasing populations. **We built mason bee**

homes (by drilling individual holes in a block of wood) and also built bumblebee houses from clay flower pots (by turning them upside down, attaching a small piece of wood to lift them off the ground, and filling them with some type of bedding material the bees won't get tangled up in-we used wool from our sheep, but you could use any type of animal hair or even dryer lint). **We also keep the borders of our property natural** by allowing the native plants to remain in their natural state (where we live, that does mean lots of brambles such as blackberry briars, but these in turn feed additional animals and us as well). **This area provides a cover for all types of wildlife** to remain hidden from our domestic animals and other predictors.

Places to Raise Young: This is the final element in a backyard habitat. We have traditional bird houses including bluebird houses, a purple martin house and some wren-size houses. This past summer, **Mia wanted to have her own garden area, so she raised birdhouse gourds.** We will dry them out to make into houses in the spring. There are lots of good reference materials available, with instructions on the size of the openings for different bird species. We also have **a squirrel nest box** in the woods behind our house and **a bat house** on the edge of our garden. The bats eat mosquitoes and fertilize our garden at the same time. **We provide nesting material for other birds** that would choose to build their own nests. We took wire suet feeders and old orange produce bags and filled them with dryer lint and animal hair (finally, a use for all the loose hair our dog and cats produce!).

That covers the basic elements you need to get your habitat certified with the National Wildlife Federation.

Mia has recently said she wants to be a scientist and she has the makings of a future entomologist

(collecting and identifying bugs is her favorite pastime). Along with the gourds she grew, she planted sunflowers so she could "feed the little birdies." She also chose to plant an apple tree and a pine tree. She checks on them daily and waters them when necessary to "help them grow big and strong." Although Mia is very young, she does many things to "help the earf" (earth). Wouldn't it be great if everyone thought that way!

Water Tips
From Carrol Wolverton
Living Cheap and Loving It: tomatoes in the flower bed

•	Run the dishwasher only when full. It's okay to partially open the door during the dry cycle and let the dishes air-dry.

•	Wash laundry in cold or tepid water, and wash full loads. Per the same Energy Star source, hot water uses 90% of the energy in washing clothes.

•	Use a low-flow showerhead. I purchased mine
for 50 cents at a garage sale. The seller didn't like the water flow. If it saves money, I like the water flow.

World Water Crisis Will Soon Reach America
By Jill A. Vanderwood

What's It Like, Living Green?

By the year 2050, over half of the world's population will be facing extreme water shortages. In the United States, people living in the states of Arizona and Nevada could be facing severe freshwater shortages by 2025.
NASA and the World Health Organization (WHO)
Sixwise.com

What is the Cause of this Shortage?

- The population of the world tripled in the 20th century, and is expected to continue growing by another 40-50 percent in the next fifty years.
- The use of water resources has increased six-fold.
- There's no more fresh water in the world today than there was 1 million years ago.
- Although petroleum can be replaced by alternative fuel sources, there is no replacement for water.
Sixwise.com

What Are the Main Sources of Fresh Water?

- Oceans, seas and bays
- Icecaps glaciers and permanent snow
- Ground water
- Soil moisture
- Ground ice and permafrost
- Lakes=fresh: 21,830 cubic miles; saline: 20,490 cubic miles
- Atmosphere
- Swamp water
- Rivers
- Biological water

USGS Science for a Changing World

Rivers

Most of our fresh water comes from rivers. Rivers, streams and creeks are all names for water that flows on the earth's surface. Rivers are formed mostly from rain or snow runoff. This water runs from the ground surface into the river.

Groundwater

Besides rivers, we get much of our water from ground-water, which also accumulates from rain and snow runoff, making it a renewable water source.

Groundwater seeps into the ground by making its way into cracks and spaces in sand, soil, and rocks, forming an aquifer. From the aquifer, the water is brought back to the surface naturally through springs, sometimes discharging into lakes and streams, or through a man-made well.

USGS Science for a Changing World-Earths Water Runoff

Over 1 Billion People Are Already Struggling for

Water

India is facing a severe water crisis. Experts predict groundwater supplies in some areas will be gone in five to ten years. This would greatly affect their food supply, turning farmland to desert. In the Middle East, Israel's former water commissioner, Meir Ben Meir, made the statement, "At the moment, I project the scarcity of water within five years." That was the year 2000.

Although China has water supplies equal to that of Canada, the population is one hundred times larger. Over half of the Chinese cities regularly face moderate to serious water shortages; each year their country will use 30 cubic kilometers more water than the rain replaces.

Water Wars

It is almost certain that once water supplies become scarcer, conflict will break out across the globe.

Maude Barlow, chair of the Council of Canadians, told the Christian Science Monitor, "water rights will be grabbed up in much the same way as the world's oil supply."

According to Meir, speaking about the Middle East, "I can promise that if there is not sufficient water in our region, and people remain thirsty for water, we shall doubtless face war,".

Sixwise.com-World Water Crisis in America and the World

Water Shortages Reach America

Although people in the US are not currently suffering as in other parts of the world, the seven states that share water from the Colorado River (Colorado, Wyoming, Utah, New Mexico, Arizona, Nevada and California) have begun negotiations on how to manage the river's limited water. The states of California, Nevada and Arizona are looking for alternative water sources while the other four states in the treaty don't want to give up their shares in the Colorado River, for fear that in case of a drought, they too may face a water shortage.

Arizona uses groundwater as well as the Colorado River for their water sources. This is an arid state and will soon be facing water shortage. They have 200 golf courses, which are using recycled water to keep them green. This state is considering treatment plants to further treat the used water, or **desalination**—removing salt from ocean water.

Naked Science Forum-Does Arizona Risk Running out of Water?

The state of **California is currently getting 30% of their water from ground water;** the rest of their water comes from the Colorado River. America and the rest of the world depend on California to grow food. Without water, there would be a severe food shortage. California also depends on the northwest for their power. With climate change or low rainfall, they could also face a power shortage.

Planning ahead, **California has proposed the building of a desalination plant,** to be built in Long Beach. Hawaii has already begun building such a plant on the islands. The main drawback is the extreme cost involved.

California is already using recycled water for outdoor landscaping, golf courses and recreation areas. To use recycled water in homes, they would need to have two separate pipes; one for fresh water and one for recycled water.

California Draught Preparedness
http://www.cadroughtprep.net/watshort.htm

From the February 20, 2006 issue of High Country News

Nevada receives only 4% of the water from the Colorado River. They currently take most of their water from Lake Mead, the home of the Hoover Dam,

which supplies most of the power for the state of Nevada. If the water level falls too low, they will also risk the loss of electricity. Online Casino Sphere-Angela Bedford

Nevada is considering desalination, in which the water would need to be piped into Nevada from California or Mexico. They are also making a switch to produce some of their power through wind power.

What are the main uses of water?

An extreme amount of water is wasted with irrigation practices throughout the world. The World Water Council points out that 66 percent of water withdrawals are for irrigation and in arid regions, 90 percent of water withdrawals go to irrigation. Water used for industry equals 20 percent and household use amounts to 10 percent. About 4 percent evaporates from reservoirs.

The key to preserving the world's limited water supply is reducing waste.
Sixwise.com

Earth Mender Tips
By Lynn Hassleburger
MyEarth360.com

Take a Green Leap!

Here are ten simple ways Earth Menders help the planet while helping their parents and teachers, too.

· **Turn off the lights** - conserves energy, cuts down on pollution and saves money on your parents' electric/light bulb bills

· **Catch the bus** - cuts down on air pollution, conserves gas and saves your parents time and gas money

· **Clean your plate and eat leftovers** - Cuts back on energy used for agriculture and keeps your parents' grocery bills down

· **Pick up your toys from the yard** - Helps your parents and the toys will last longer

· **Pick up your clothes.** They'll last longer, saving your parents money... Plus, if you keep them clean, you can often wear them again, cutting back on chemicals, energy and water used to wash them

· **Put your own paper and plastic in the recycle bin** - keeps your room clean and cuts down on landfill waste

· **Pick up trash in your yard or around the school** - tidies the grounds and keeps trash from entering our soil and waterways

· **Don't beg for fast food** - saves your parents money and cuts back on disposable waste

· **Pass down sibling's clothes** - cuts down on

the budget, cuts back on energy and resources needed to produce and ship new clothing

·   **Turn off the water** - cuts down on water/water
softening/water heater bills while conserving our natural resources

America Has the Ability
to Feed the World
Tammie Umbel
Mother of Eleven Children
Owner of Shea Terra Organics
sheaterraorganics.com

The area surrounding my ten-acre, organically-man-
aged farm in Leesburg, VA is a picture I have seen
again and again in my travels across the country. What
used to be cow pastures and cash crop farms are now
miniature luxury estates. Across from a five-hundred-
acre cow farm are houses over ten thousand square
feet with five to twenty acres apiece. While the owners of these houses look
outside to their kingdom of
lush, manicured "pastures,"
I see endless waste.

**America has the abil-
ity to feed the world, yet
landowners allow their
lots to lay idle** rather than
leasing them to others to
cultivate. Virginia can grow

more varieties of food than anywhere in the US, being able to grow things of both southern and northern climates. **We grow mighty good apples and darned good grapes, yet these foods are being imported en masse from countries with no regard for human safety or environment.** Tons of pesticides are sprayed on the food imported into the US, many that are banned on food produced in the US. Countries such as China do not have the strict environmental regulations or fair labor laws the US has, but we still choose to import their food.

Things are not hopeless; each one of us has the power to change the path we are on. I will start off by telling you a few things we do on our homestead and give a few suggestions for those who may have little to no property of their own.

Our whole family gets involved in the process of running our farm. We are connected with the land and ourselves. Our organic farming practice, not unlike our forefathers', provides nutrition not found in stores. We eat plants at their peak energy levels. **We appreciate what we eat, and we get plenty of exercise.** Studies have proven that gardening is mentally therapeutic, and I could not agree more.

Chickens- From our chickens we get a steady supply of nutrition. I do have eleven children, so it should not come as any surprise that we also have around seventy chickens. Our chickens go into their coop to roost at night and we let them out to range during the day. Besides a steady diet of bugs and weeds,

we give them some grain with calcium and our table scraps. Keeping our own chickens ensures that our hens are not living miserable lives so we can enjoy our breakfast. And, every egg is packed with vital nutrition for growing children.

Cows- We do have a few cows for milk, but I won't go into this as it is not easy for everyone to do.

Organic, edible landscaping- Instead of filling our property with plants that merely look good, and often times require a lot of chemicals to maintain, we plant kiwi, figs, blueberries, and the like. **I have a saying: if it doesn't produce food, I don't want it.** We have almost one hundred fruit trees- apples, pears, cherries, pomegranates, and plums. We never buy pre-squeezed, processed juices from the store. We only drink juice we squeeze fresh so we can assure the juice keeps all of its qualities. Fruit we don't consume becomes juice and any leftovers go to neighbors. The great thing about apples is that they can be stored for several months.

Organic garden- I find it essential to get as much fresh, green food as possible. Even if we cannot produce all of our own food, we can produce some that will provide us with vital immune-enhancing nutrients. There are even ways of gardening greens year round.

Sheep- We fence as much land as we can and keep baby doll sheep on it. They are particularly good in orchards. Not only do they make great lawn mowers and weed killers, they are also so cute.

What you can do:

1) **Community chickens**—if you have land zoned for agriculture, consider keeping a few chickens. If your community won't allow farm animals, get your neighbors together to petition for the county to allow

Take a
Green
Leap!

backyard chickens. Three chickens are easy to clean up after and they make very little noise. Contrary to popular belief, a rooster is not required to produce eggs.

Or petition for a community chicken lot. Several neighbors can go together to raise free-range chickens and share the eggs. Raising chickens is a particularly great project for families with children. This will insure that your eggs are fresh and the chickens are healthy.

2) **Community orchards**- Petition your local government to fill empty lots with trees. Trees clean the air and provide homes to birds that control insects. Fruit trees would make the best choice. Community members can band together to take care of the trees. Fruit can be divided and leftovers can go to homeless shelters or elderly homes. The elderly, particularly those living at poverty level, can greatly benefit from the nutrition fresh fruits provide.

3) **Grass**- You can petition your local government to grow plants that do not require cutting. There are quite a few varieties. For larger lots of unused grass, petition your government to allow the citizens to produce their own food. These lots can be planted with perennials like asparagus, strawberries and blueberries.

4) **Sheep**- Wherever possible, raise sheep, goats or cows to keep your grass under control.

5) **Edible landscaping**-There are several decorative food plants that can replace existing non-food producing plants. Blueberries make beautiful shrubs for

the front yard, as do gooseberries. Strawberries make great borders. Cranberries make attractive, edible groundcovers (you don't need a bog to grow cranberries).

6) **Got land?** Please, pretty please, if you have land, lease it to others who yearn to farm it. If you have a lawn, it can be grown for hay. There are hay companies who will come out and bail it for you. You get a government tax write-off plus possibly save money for land use tax.

7) **Grow your own garden-** You don't need a yard to grow a garden. Every bit counts. You can even grow your own arugula and herbs in your windows. A bucket is all you need to grow tomatoes on your porch. If you do have a yard, even a tiny one, consider some raspberry plants. They are a potent cancer fighter. You might also consider a few small garden boxes. I highly recommend http://www.squarefootgardening.com/.

8) **Buy local-** Patronize farmers growing locally. Be willing to pay a little more. Don't ask, demand (in a civilized way, of course) your local stores to carry more local food. If it is September and you live where apples are grown, let stores know your displeasure that they are importing apples. Are they going to be more expensive? Yes, but it is a spiral effect. It really comes down to supply and demand.

9) **Avoid imported produce-** Stop buying foods that come from countries with questionable farming practices. Ban such foods and let your local stores know how you feel. You will be amazed what one person can

do. Educate your friends, and they will start doing the same.

Remember, you might not be able to produce all your food. But **every plant you grow decreases the amount of land cut down in the rainforest to sustain you.** Gardening makes a person whole. It provides much-needed exercise and even improves flexibility. It is good for everyone. Children benefit, the elderly benefit, and everyone in between.

6
Kids Teaching Kids, by the Way They Live

"I know that children everywhere can make a difference in their own communities and beyond. ....Get noticed for doing something positive."
Devon Green

Ryan's Well Organization
Ryan Hreljac
North Grenville, Ontario, Canada

Ryan and Jimmy in Uganda

Ryan is a compelling and passionate voice for those impacted by the water crisis in the developing world. He continues to be a role model with a clear message—that every person on the planet deserves clean water, and one voice (the power of one) can make a huge difference.

When you turn on the water faucet in your home, what do you expect to happen? Most likely either hot or cold water will come out, splashing into the sink and running down the drain. You can also expect the water to be clean.

What if you lived in a village where there was no clean water? What if your home didn't even have a kitchen or bathroom sink, a tub or even a toilet?

In 1998, when Ryan Hreljac was in the first grade, he learned from his teacher, Mrs. Prest, that people were dying because they didn't have clean water to drink.

"Wait until you're older," or "You're too young." Do these statements sound familiar? They didn't stop Ryan. He decided to raise money for people who didn't have clean water. This six-year-old boy worked for four months in order to earn his first $70. Most children would change their minds about all the hard work, or find something else to buy with the money, but not Ryan. He continued to fund-raise and used his hard-earned money to build his first well at a school in a Ugandan village. Built in 1999, the well continues to serve thousands of people. With this accomplishment, Ryan's determination continued to grow. From the $70, collected by doing simple household chores, grew a Foundation that today has contributed a total of **461 wells in 16 countries**, bringing clean water and sanitation service to over **599,081 people**. The Foundation has raised millions of dollars.

Now at age seventeen, Ryan completed the 11th grade with the Class Afloat program. He spent part of the year at school on the east coast of Canada (Lunenburg, Nova Scotia) and the second half (February -July) on a tall ship, getting his education while sailing around the world. **Ryan is joined by his family as he continues to speak passionately about the need for clean water.** He visits countries such as Argentina, Brazil,

Ryan at His First Well, Nine Years Later

South Africa, the Dominican Republic, and Namibia. Ryan will complete his last year of high school at home in North Grenville.

Being recognized by UNICEF as a Global Youth Leader, Ryan enjoys speaking to schools, churches, civic clubs and more than two dozen international conferences, including Rotary International and the World Water Forums.

Ryan's older brother, Jordan ,works on the Foundation's Global Youth Initiative and also makes presentations on behalf of the Foundation. His younger brother Keegan is the Foundation's photographer and gives presentations to youth. His Ugandan pen pal, Jimmy Akana, who Ryan met on his first trip to the country, is now part of the Hreljac family. He also makes presentations on behalf of the Ryan's Well Foundation around the world.

Ryan has received many awards for his work, including the *World of Children Founders'* Award, the *Order of Ontario* (youngest-ever recipient), *Ontario Medal for Young Volunteers*, the *Canadian Meritorious Service Medal*, and the *Top 20 under 20 Youth Award*. His message has been featured on the *Oprah Winfrey Show* (twice), CNN, and CBC. Numerous books, magazines and newspapers have profiled Ryan, including the *Christian Science Monitor, People Magazine,* the *Reader's Digest, Time Magazine, Times of London* and *Watervoices.*

Although Ryan has met some of the most important people in the world, he says, **"The most impressive people I've met are the other kids who want to help, too."** When anyone asks about his achievements, he answers, "I'm just your regular, average kid." This is very true. He enjoys playing basketball, participating in ice hockey, and loves to play video games.

The next time you hear, "You're too young," or the question, "How can you make a difference?" add your voice to that of Ryan and other kids around the world. Go out and **make a difference.**

Here's how others have taken a Green Leap and helped Ryan's Well Foundation make sure everyone has clean water!

Take a Green Leap!

Youth Initiatives
Children are:
•   Asking for donations to Ryan's Well, rather than birthday presents
•   Asking for donations to Ryan's Well, rather than Christmas gifts
•   Having Bat Mitzvah parties to educate people about the importance of clean water and taking donations for Ryan's Well, rather than receiving gifts
•   A Cub Scout troop raised money by doing chores, donating allowance, recycling cans, and selling Halloween candy
•   Donating one month's allowance
•   Raising money by having a lemonade stand
•   One girl set up a money jar with a sign at her dad's work
•   Another girl set up a wishing well at school, charging $0.25 to make a wish
Schools Have Donated to Ryan's Well by:
•   Chore-a-thon or Read-a-thon
•   Auction—which can involve donated gifts from businesses in the community
•   Recycling projects

103

- One school collected loose change every Friday for a whole year
- Pancake breakfast
- A week of fund-raising—the top fund-raiser got to "pie" their teacher

Devon's Heal the World Recycling
Giving Back

By Devon Green
From Florida

Since starting my recycling business when I was five years old, **I have consistently donated my earnings and time to help others in my community.**

I volunteered my time for many charities, but I have also sponsored my own fund-raisers to benefit my community on four separate occasions. In 2001, I donated my tenth birthday to the Humane Society and did a self-orchestrated fund-raiser for them. This resulted

104

in $3,500.00 raised for the construction of a new shelter and several tons of pet supplies donated.

On January 12, 2002, I was given the honor of cutting the ribbon at the grand opening of the new Humane Society complex that I had helped to make possible.

In 2002, I donated my eleventh birthday to The Hibiscus Children's Center. I raised $8,000 to purchase new bunk beds for the kids, and my secondary goal was to save their "Crisis Nursery" program. My final tally for that fund-raiser was over $80,000.00. During the 2002 holiday season, I raised another $14,000 for the Humane Society to sponsor pet adoptions. I also worked with my generous community and an anonymous matching donor to raise over $170,000 for Hibiscus Children's Center that was used to sponsor the visitation center in the "Hibiscus Children's Village" in Vero Beach, Florida. These four fund-raisers resulted in nearly $275,000.00 being raised for charity.

During the spring of 2003, I helped my sister to organize a toy drive for the shelter kids at the Hibiscus Children's Center.

Following in my footsteps, six-year-old Jessie donated her birthday to bring smiles to the faces of the abused and neglected children served at the shelter. Most recently, I helped Jessie to celebrate her ninth birthday by serving as an advisor during her fund-raiser for ARC of Martin County and The Humane Society.

Jessie and I both believe in leading by example, so we both contribute our money as well as our time to all of our fund-raising events. I also donated the $500.00 community service award that I received from Sheriff Robert Crowder on June 17, 2003 to the Treasure Coast Wildlife Hospital.

We have spoken to numerous groups of children in my community including school classrooms, church

105

groups, boys and girls clubs, and Girl Scouts on topics such as goal setting, the value of recycling, and the importance of sharing and giving back to one's community.

For the past six years, Jessie and I have been volunteering our time as pet therapists for the local Humane Society. We visit nursing homes and also participate in the *Paws to Read* program, where children practice reading to our well-trained therapy cats, Pretty Boy, Sweetie, and Suki.

I am currently seventeen years old and have no interest in slowing down in my mission to "Heal The World." Jessie is eleven, and I know she feels the same as I do about our efforts.

We have been recognized by Keep Martin Beautiful, The Palm City Chamber of Commerce, the Martin County School Board, the U.S. Small Business Administration, the Association of Fund Raising Professionals, the Humane Society of the Treasure Coast, Hibiscus Children's Center, and the Martin County Sheriff's Office with special awards to recognize our contributions to the community.

In 2002, I was selected by Sears as their national kid

hero, and in 2003, Georgia Pacific selected me as one of their ten nationwide "Angels In Action."

The "good news" about just how much one kid can accomplish is spreading fast through the media both here in the United States and abroad. Our story has been shared through *The New York Times*, *The London Financial Times*, *The Times of London*, *El Pais Magazine of Madrid*, and *Luna Magazine of Italy*. Also, the media in France has expressed an interest in doing a documentary about us for French TV, and third grade children in the Netherlands are learning English by reading the story of "Devon's Heal The World Recycling" in their language textbook.

My primary job at this time is that of college student. I recently received my A.A. degree Suma Cum Laude from Indian River State College. I have been accepted as a junior transfer student at Western Carolina University and will soon begin my enrollment.

I hope that I have and will continue to inspire other kids and young adults that I meet locally and around the world to get involved in their communities and get noticed for doing something positive.

I know that **children everywhere can make a difference** in their own communities and beyond. By reading and hearing about Jessie and me, they are all being empowered to use their energy for something positive to make a difference for themselves and for others.

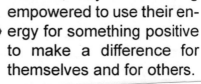

You Can **Take A Green Leap!** To help your community.

Both Jessie and I went through certain steps,

learning to raise money for good causes.

1) In the beginning, I would go door-to-door to businesses in strip malls or office buildings. I went wherever I was allowed to solicit donations.

2) I stood outside grocery stores, libraries—anywhere there was a lot of walking traffic. However, I never solicited in residential neighborhoods, because I didn't really feel that was appropriate.

3) The next step was to design an attractive flier and donation form explaining what I was trying to accomplish. This would include the logo (with permission) of the organization I was raising money for. This added credibility to my venture.

4) Soon the money I was trying to raise became too much to accomplish going door-to-door speaking to one or two people at a time. As a member of the Chamber of Commerce, I was able to get a list of all the civic organizations in our community. I began to call them and set up speaking opportunities. Now I was speaking to 50, 75, or 100 people at a time, so raising larger amounts of money became more possible.

5) The next step was adding visual aids to my presentations, such as display boards telling about and showing pictures of those we wanted to help and what we wanted to provide for them.

6) We took an additional step by contacting the local media and asking for their help. Sometimes they would tell our story, and sometimes they would actually show up to cover one of my speaking opportunities. Jessie did go through all the steps so she could see how each one added to our success, but she was able to move through the steps much quicker than I did, because I already knew what worked best and was able to guide her.

A Girl with a Plan
Jessica Green
Age 11

Parties, candles, bal- loons, and presents are a normal part of a nine- year-old's birthday, right? Jessica Green had other plans for her birthday. **She set a goal to raise $10,000** to provide hurri- cane survival kits for ARC and the Humane Society. Jessie says, "We need to plan for those who can't plan for themselves in case we get hit by another storm."

The kits provide food, water, shelter, medical sup- plies, and miscellaneous necessities for an ARC client or a Humane Society pet during and after a storm. Jes- sie's plan was to provide forty kits at $250.00 each. Twenty survival kits were to be donated to ARC, and twenty to the Humane Society.

With her older sister Devon as an advisor, Jessie visited government officials and organizations in her Martin County Florida community. At times, **the small girl with a big heart had to stand on a chair just to be seen.** She needed the help of a microphone to be heard, but her message got through.

Jessica not only raised her goal amount of $10,000, but with matching donations from the community, the total amount was $11,528. How did she do it? By sharing a table with the Humane Society at the Hurricane Fair, going door-to-door and speaking to groups of people wherever they would listen to her presentation. Stuart Sunrise Rotary club, two Kiwanis clubs, Business Network International, Smith Barney, and the County Commissioners were among the groups who allowed her to come in and talk with them.

For her eleventh birthday, Jessie set the bar even higher. Her presentation to the Rotary Club included a freehand drawing of her proposed playground for the Hibiscus Children's Center. Her plan was to raise $30,000 to cover the cost of **a safe and exciting playground for the kids at the shelter.** She hopes the new playground will include a safe rubberized foundation, slides, swings, ladders, tunnels, a water feature, and lots of other fun stuff. The playground will also include a "hero wall" where the names of contributors who made it all possible will be engraved, compliments of Mike's Trophies in Stuart, Florida.

Jessica planned to make her presentation to civic groups, church groups, and clubs throughout her community. With the help of Devon, so far Jessie has been able to raise about $7,000 of the $30,000 needed to build the new playground for the Hibiscus Children's shelter. This project has been moving slower than anticipated because of the weak economy, but she is optimistic that she will succeed in reaching her goal. She has already solicited contributions from local businesses for a fence around the playground, a water feature

 in the playground area and the before-mentioned hero's wall. The staff at the shelter has been in touch with Jessie to let her know that there are some additional contributions forthcoming that will help her complete this project and make the new playground a reality.

Jessie and Devon were hoping to have the playground completed in time to be a Christmas present for the shelter kids, but now they expect to have it completed by early 2009.

Kids Saving the Rainforest
By Janine Licare
Co-Founder and Spokesperson for
Kids Saving the Rainforest

OUR PLEDGE!
We believe that the rainforest is a storehouse of treasures. We vow to do everything we can to save it. With the vanishing rainforest goes the future of our planet. We have to be the generation which makes a difference!

"Rocks for sale! Come and buy some pretty rocks!"

111

Nine-year-old Janine Licare and her friend Aislin Livingstone spent a sunny afternoon in their beautiful rainforest of Manuel Antonio, Costa Rica, searching for smooth rocks to paint with brightly colored designs.

While the paint dried on their art treasures, they set up a roadside stand on the edge of Janine's yard.

With paint smudges on their hands and clothing, the girls set to work selling their beautiful works of art. They planned to earn their own spending money.

"Within just a few days, we knew we should put to use what we earned for something much more important. That's when we had the idea to start saving the rainforest."

Together with Janine's mother, Jennifer Rice, the girls started "Kids Saving the Rainforest" in 1998. In 1999, the girls' idea took off when they opened the "Kids Saving the Rainforest" store. Today, the successful store not only sells children's artwork, but also the work of local artists and craftspeople, and KSTR merchandise. This store also serves as an information source about the organization and environmental issues. One hundred percent of the proceeds go to save the rainforest.

"Ever since we were little, we acknowledged the fact that the rainforest is home to many kinds of animals as well as other living organisms, such as trees, plants and insects. The rainforest is an amazing place and we vow to do anything and everything we can to save it. It is very important that we preserve the environment because by saving it, we make sure our future is protected and available for the next generations. If it disappears, then so does our planet.

We've worked diligently over the last several years to make a difference."

This is a juvenile male titi monkey. He was brought to us after being confiscated by MINAE. The people who owned him either wanted to keep him as a pet or sell him on the black market. He's healthy, but doesn't have a troop to live with, in the wild.

KSTR has purchased four acres of rainforest property where we built an animal rehabilitation center in which we care for and release injured and abandoned animals. We have saved and released 50 animals so far!

KSTR has erected and maintains more than 130 monkey bridges that are used by monkeys and other animals so they don't get hit by cars when crossing roads, nor electrocuted by using power lines.

KSTR has a reforestation program in which we have planted over 6000 trees to reforest and to create monkey corridors.

KSTR has a Saturday kid's camp where we teach local and visiting kids about the rainforest and its destruction, and then we empower them to save it.

KSTR has sister schools and members all around the world, including countries such as India, Denmark, Vietnam, England, Pakistan, France, Canada, USA, and Costa Rica.

KSTR has a program within our community and in the Manuel Antonio national park where we teach the public about the importance of not feeding the monkeys.

KSTR has a public library (the first in the area) with over 2500 books people can borrow.

KSTR has published three children's books that are being sold to the public.

"With the help of volunteers, friends, classmates, and the community, we've come a long way.

"I believe kids can make a real difference. With your help, there's no limit as to how far we can go! Join us and do your part in saving the world!"
Tropically yours,
Janine Licare

CLASSROOM ACTIVITIES

Goal: to educate students about the rainforests and its endangered state and to empower them to be active participants in saving the rainforests.

OBJECTIVES:

- Students will learn about the plants, trees, and animals found within the rainforests of Manuel Antonio.
- Children will present their knowledge of the rainforests through a variety of works. (Students could create artwork, poems, essays, songs, maps, collages, etc.)
- Students will raise money for the rainforests of Manuel Antonio by incorporating their acquired knowledge and their works. Ideas for carrying out the objectives:

#1. Students will compile their work and create a calendar, featuring all they have learned. Students will have a chance to feature their work and hopefully they themselves will be featured as well. Your calendars may even be created with the help of a color copier or scanner. You may wish to work on the finishing touches with the help of a professional. They could be sold within the school, the community, or at a local business. The proceeds can go to help save the rainforest.

 # 2. Students will gather artwork that will then be sold to raise money. Hosting an art gallery allows students to sell their work for the purpose of profiting the rainforests. The gallery itself draws positive attention to the students, teachers, and schools that are partaking in a good cause. An art gallery can be hosted in the school, shopping mall, grocery store, or any place that draws in a lot of people.

#3. Students will write to local businesses, asking them to make a donation to sponsor a particular plant or tree found within the rainforests of Manuel Antonio. When students interact with local businesses, they will learn the value of interacting with society as a whole. It is our hope that through this interaction, students will realize the impact one voice can have.

#4. Students will contact local media (newspapers, radio stations, television stations, etc.) so the community may be made aware of their efforts in raising money. Involving the media brings increased awareness and support from your community. Your classrooms' involvement and efforts will be amplified, drawing respect and appreciation for all your students have done.

The founders of "Kids Saving the Rainforest" are excited about interacting with schools from around the world. With the help of teachers and students like you who have discovered our mission, we can save the rainforests of Manuel Antonio. The activities we suggest provide an opportunity for students to not only learn, but to make a real difference!

Kids for A Clean Environment
By Melissa Poe, Founder Of Kids F.A.C.E.

Kids F.A.C.E. is the world's largest youth environmental organization - much more than the first six members who gathered at Percy Priest Elementary in Nashville, Tennessee in 1989.

Melissa Poe is proof that kids can make a difference. There are many TV shows that teach kids to be responsible for the earth, such as the environmental initiative on Nickelodeon, the Big Green Help. At nine years old, after viewing an episode of Highway to Heaven, Melissa began to think, "What will the future world be like

116

if we don't help take care of the environment today?" At the end of the program, however, Michael Landon, the actor, said "It's not too late. People who care will do something!"

Not wanting to grow up in a world with a polluted environment, **Melissa decided she wanted to be one of those who cared.** She started Kids F.A.C.E. as a club for all the kids who cared about the environment and wanted to be involved in making a change.

"Club members started doing things like recycling, picking up litter, and planting trees as well as inviting other kids to join their club. Soon, letters written by kids started arriving, with questions like: 'How can I help ...what can I do... how can I join your club and get started saving the  environment?' The more people heard about the club, the more people wanted to join and do things for the environment."

As the club began to grow, Melissa Poe found that there were real bills to pay, which is something most kids don't need to worry about. Mail poured in from around the world, and it would require time for letter writing as well as postage stamps. Having a newsletter would solve that problem by giving the club a way to communicate with all the new members.

"The organization was established 'by kids and for kids' but to continue, some very special adults would have to come forward and help.

After writing to Sam Walton, the owner/founder of the Wal-Mart Corporation, asking for help, he and Wal-

Mart adopted Kids F.A.C.E.. In 1990, Kids F.A.C.E. was incorporated as a non-profit organization.

"This partnership has made it possible for any child who wants to get involved with their community and help protect nature to join the club free of charge.

"Now, membership is over 300,000 strong all across the United States and in twenty-two foreign countries." Melissa Poe

 *The mission of Kids for a Clean Environment is to provide information on environmental issues to children, to encourage and facilitate youths' involvement with effective environmental action and to recognize those efforts which result in the improvement of nature.*

- **Kids F.A.C.E.® translated =** Kids (F)or (A) (C)lean (E)nvironment.
- **The creation of Kids F.A.C.E. was driven by Melissa's correspondence to then-president Bush to help clean up the environment. Over 250 billboards with Melissa's letter to the president were placed across the United States in April, 1990.**
- **First chapter of the club was formed in Hattiesburg, Mississippi, in 1990 after Melissa's appearance on the TODAY show. Following that appearance, the organization started to grow.**
- **Today there are more than <u>2,000 club chapters in fifteen countries.</u> The organization is the world's largest youth environmental organization. Membership is free to children and teachers.**

•   Kids F.A.C.E. members have distributed and planted over <u>1 million</u> trees. Ongoing tree-planting projects include the creation of Kid's Yards - backyard wildlife habitats and currently Kids F.A.C.E. is involved in the exciting Earth Odyssey.

•   <u>Kids F.A.C.E. members created the world's largest environmental flag - measuring 100' x 200'</u> - to symbolize the concerns youth have about nature and the future world. The flag was unveiled during the twenty-fifth celebration of Earth Day in Washington, D.C.

•   Kids F.A.C.E. has received national awards for its youth environmental projects, including the "1997 A Pledge and a Promise" award for the Power of One program.

You Can Start a Chapter of Kids F.A.C.E.

In conjunction with planning youth environmental activities and associating with Kids for A Clean Environment, we ask that your programs and activities include:

•   Focus on solution, not problems, and without "pointing fingers"

•   Motivate participants to take positive actions

•   Strive for ethnic/cultural, economic, age, gender, and physical ability diversity

•   At no time be used to influence local, regional, state or national rules, policies, laws, or government officials

•   All chapters will remain totally at the discretion and pleasure of you and your participants.

119

- We will provide membership packets, membership certificates program material, ideas, brochures, etc.
- You are welcome to:
  - use anything we send you in its entirety, if it serves your needs
  - use the Kids F.A.C.E.® name with your activities, as long as you agree to our guidelines
  - use the Kids F.A.C.E ® logo upon written request, and
  - submit articles and information about your activities for distribution through our network
- For more information on limited permission, permission to use the logo and an application form, visit www.kidsface.org -- Start Your Chapter page

Kids F.A.C.E.
P.O. Box 158254
Nashville, Tennessee 37215
Telephone: 615-331-7381

Creating a Green School
By Susan Rys
Principal: St. Benedict School
Blue Island, IL

Earth Odyssey
Kids F.A.C.E.
For a Clean Environment

Student Pledge

I pledge as a Catholic School Student to conserve energy and defend from waste and overuse the natural
resources of God's Creation – its soils, forests and wildlife. I pledge to reduce, renew, and reuse resources
whenever possible. I pledge to help maintain clean air
and water. I pledge to change my lifestyle to improve
the quality of life from a green point of view. I pledge to
teach others about ways to help save the environment.
I pledge to be a caretaker to the environment and all of
the goodness of God's creation. Amen.
Written by Jerry Martinez and Patrick Kennedy

St. Benedict School in Blue Island, IL launched their Earth Odyssey on January 29, 2009. Planning for the event began in October, 2008. The school's commitment to ongoing service projects, coupled with our desire to preserve nature and the environment for kids of tomorrow, led us to this special kick off ceremony. Our commitment to "Going Green" was facilitated by Kids F.A.C.E. (www.kidsface.org), an organization formed by kids, where kids can work hard to make a difference for the future of the earth. The information on their website inspired us to launch an Earth Odyssey at our school during our Catholic Schools Week.

After Thanksgiving, 2008, each student in preschool through grade eight researched a 'green' topic and created their own project. The projects needed to include a visual display as well as a Public Service Announcement that identified a problem and the solution. Each student presented both an oral and written report, along with a visual display. The purpose of each project was to motivate others to take positive actions toward a particular environmental problem. A variety of topics were covered in each classroom, to allow students to learn from each other.

Students chose a topic from a list provided below.

Topic choices included:

- Organic Farming / Foods
- Sustainable Agri-

Empty Landfills by Diana Sanchez

culture / Fair Trade
- Energy Use/Conservation
- Alternative Sources—Hydro, Water, Wind, Solar
- Renewable vs. Fossil Fuels and electric
- Recycling, Reusing, Reducing
- Websites and Organizations Committed to the Environment
- Land Conservation
- Water Conservation
- Endangered, Threatened, or At-Risk Species
- Species Survival Plan
- Global Warming: Fact or Fiction?
- Warning Signs on Impending Problems (e.g. frogs, bees, are disappearing)
- Eco-Friendly Products
- Green Cleaning / Automobiles
- Green Architecture
- Eco-Tourism and Eco-travel Options
- Holistic Science / Herbal Remedies
- The Local Movement (Celebrities involved)
- Green Collar Jobs

In addition to the student projects, a Green Team was formed. Eight seventh graders worked with the principal, Mrs. Rys, on school-wide initiatives and campaigns, along with the planning of the Earth Odyssey Assembly. Students composed a letter and an invitation to our guests, wrote prayers, petitions, and the Student Pledge. One student wrote the lyrics for "Kids All Over the Planet." Mr. Whitaker, our music teacher, wrote the music for this special song. (The words for the song are on the last page.) Plans were also made for the ecology Kids F.A.C.E. rocket to launch at the assembly.

As the time drew closer to the launch, Confirmation

students offered their time to help with the artwork for

The Green Team
Back Row (left to right): Regina Bressanelli,
Jerry Martinez, Patrick Kennedy,
Mitch Stachulak, Ryan Barr, Elizabeth Young
Front Row: Lauren Duffy, Casey Warrick

the assembly, which included the Kids F.A.C.E. logos and rockets that highlighted our "Countdown to Earth Odyssey" and the launch date and time: January 29, 2009 at 10:00 a.m. During the week of January 25th, students brought in their projects to be displayed in the classrooms; each student had the opportunity to present their reports to their classmates.

A sampling of projects, from each classroom, was displayed for the assembly, on January 29. The mayor of Blue Island and other special guests were present to witness this historic event. Students sang "Kids All Over the Planet, shared Public Service Announcements, and recited the pledge together. After the pledge, we had our count down and launched our rocket, symbolic of our life-long commitment to preserving nature and the environment for kids of tomorrow. The mayor passed out Kids F.A.C.E. certificates to a representative of each grade level. St. Benedict School became an official chapter of Kids F.A.C.E, and every student became an official member. Our kids and our school are committed to make a difference, by preserving nature and the environment for the kids of future.

Kids All Over the Planet (song)
written by Jerry Martinez

Chorus
Kids all over the planet
We don't like waste
Why don't we just ban it?
And make this world a better place

Vs. 1
We'll find a clean place for you and me
On the land, in the air, and in the sea
We must join forces to help save this planet we love.

Chorus
Kids all over the planet
We don't like waste
Why don't we just ban it?
And make this world a better place

Vs. 2
Let's be brave
Recycle, rebuild, renew
To save this planet for me and you

Chorus

Take a
Green
Leap!

Student-generated campaigns led to the implementation of the following:
- Bins for recycling newspapers and magazines have been added.
- Recycling bins for plastic, aluminum cans and cardboard have been added.
- Recycling of ink cartridges, cell phones, CDs and DVDs will also begin.
- ACI, the recycling company in town, is going to offer scholarships for students who go above and beyond in their efforts to the preserving the environment.
- The Green Team will also feature a weekly Green Memo that will offer A to Z ideas for Going Green. This will ensure that our commitment continues beyond January, 2009.

You can also become a green school by:
- Preparing a motto for your school
- Getting everyone involved
- Teaching others by the way you live
- Joining the Earth Odyssey on www.kidsface. org:

The Earth Odyssey addresses three important environmental issues: Habitats, Air Quality and Land Management. Kids F.A.C.E. Earth Odyssey programs focus on survival of animals, the health of children and the loss of natural resources. Earth Odyssey invites you to join: Mission Recycle, Mission Build, or Mission Plant.

Answers to the Living Green Quiz

1) A is the green choice, C is the light green choice
2) B is the green choice
3) C is the green choice, B is the light green choice
4) C is the green choice, A is the light green choice
5) B is the green choice
6) B and C are both green choices
7) B and C are both green choices
8) C is the green choice *if you take a newspaper- a) share with a neighbor b) you can use the paper to wash windows c) recycle when finished*
9) B and C are both green choices
10) C is the green choice

For more information
And Other Related Topics:

Antibiotics in Milk: Milk: Does a body good? www.westenaprice.org
Preventing Antibiotic Residue in Milk: NC State University—www.cesncsu.edu Organic Valley Milk—www.organicvalley.coop

Back Yard Animal Habitats: National Wildlife Federation—www.nwf.org/gardenforwildlife/

Bottle Bills: Bottle Bill resource guide—http://www.bottlebill.org

BPA: Plastics in Our Diet: the need for BPA regulation-Scientific American—www.sciam.com/article.cfm?id=plastics_in_our_diet

Carbon Footprints: Calculate, reduce and offset—http://www.carbonfootprint.com/
The Nature Conservancy—What's Your Carbon Footprint?—http:www.nature.org/initiatives/climatechange/calculator/

Co2 emissions: Wikipedia list of countries by carbon dioxide emissions—http://en.wikipedia.org/wiki/list

Disposable Diapers: The Great Disposable Diaper Debate—Sustainability Institute.org
sustainabilityinstitute.org

Fair Trade: Labeling Organization International—http://www.fairtrade.net

Global Warming: US EPA Global Warming Site: http://www.epa.gov/climatechange/ EPA Global Warming kids site; Wikipedia.com

Green Cleaning Products: SC Johnson Wax--SC Johnson.com; The Cleaning Authority—TheCleaningAuthority.com; Seventh Generation — Seventhgerneration.com/products; Arm and Hammer products — rmandhammeressentials.com

Green Cosmetics: Zosimos Botanicals—*StartupNation deems Zosimos Botanicals one of the Top 10 Greenest Home-Based Businesses of 2008.* www.Zosimosbotanicals.com
Simmons Naturals—www.simmonsnaturals.com
Shea Terra Organics—www.sheaterraorganics.com

Greenhouse Gasses: Wikipedia—http://en.wikipedia.org/wiki/greenhouse_gas
Greenhouse Gasses—http://www.umich.edugs265/society/greenhouse.htm

High Fructose Corn Syrup: The Murky World of High Fructose Corn Syrup—http://www.westonaprice.org/motherlinda/cornsyrup.html
High Fructose Corn Syrup: what are the concerns? Mayoclinc.com

Hormones in Meat: Avoiding Hormones in Meat and Poultry—Beef and Lamb have hormones added, (the US does not allow hormones in pork, chicken, turkey or fouls)—From Dr. Weil—www.drweil.com/drw/u/idQAA400066
American Beef: Why is it banned in Europe? Cancer

Prevention Coalition— (hormone levels in meat are mostly unregulated). uhttp://www.preventcancer.com/consumers/general/hormones_meat.htm

Hybrid Cars: Information about Hybrid Vehicles—www.hybridcars.com
The New Gas-Electric Hybrid Cars—http://www.earth-easy.com/live_hybrid_car.htm

Hydro Power: Energy Kids Page—Energy Information Administration—EIA Hydropower-Water Energy—http://www.eia.doe.gov/kids/energyfacts/sources/renewable/water.html

Mercury in Fish: US Environmental Protection Agency Fish Advisories—five common fish low in mercury are: shrimp, canned light tuna, Pollock, and catfish—eat two fish meals per week. White albacore tuna is higher in mercury. EPA.org

Organic: Organic foods are made according to certain production standards—without pesticides.
http://enWikipedia.org/wiki/organic_food
News, articles, recipes, product reviews on organic food--http://www.organic.org/
Pesticides: About pesticides: most pesticides create some risk. http://www.epa.gov/pesticides/about

Recycled paper: Information on recycled paper from California Integrated waste management—http://www.ciwmb.ca.gov/paper/recycled

Renewable Energy Sources: Energy Kids Page---Energy Information Administration—
http://www.eia.doe.gov/kids/energyfacts/sources/re-

newable/renewable.htm/

Tree Free Paper: Paper Home: Information on tree-free paper compiled by the California Integrated Waste Management Board—http://www.ciwmb.ca.gov/paper/TreeFree/

Vegan: Vegan Action is a nonprofit organization that educates the public about the many benefits of a Vegan diet and lifestyle—http://www.vegan.org/vegan.com—Articles, interviews, product evaluations and book reviews

Vegetarian: Sites differences between vegetarians and vegans—http://en.wikipedia.org/wiki/vegetarian-ism

Water Pollution: Concise introduction of different types of water pollution, including causes and effects---http://www.umich.edu/~gs265/society/waterpollution.htm

Water Shortages: What is water pollution? http://www.geocites.com/RainForest/516/water1.htm

Wild Life: National Wildlife Federation—NWF's mission is to inspire Americans to protect wildlife for our children's future—Information and application for a backyard preserve.
http://www.nwf.org/

Contributors to
What's It Like, Living Green?
Kids Teaching Kids,
by the Way They Live

Azura Ammon is a sixteen-year-old home schooled student from Albany Ohio, who has been raised to be environmentally conscious.

Jeanette Ammon is the mother of two and a Healing Touch Message Therapist from Albany, Ohio. Jeanette teaches us how to walk gently on this mother earth.

Wynne Coplea is an environmental educator from Springfield, Illinois, who teaches kids how to live green, use less water, electricity and create less waste.

Alexandra Gnoske Davila is the mother of two children who lives in North Chicago, Illinois. Alix is teaching her children and other parents to reuse, reduce and recycle.
President/Founding Member
RECYCLE ME
Organic Cotton Clothing
alix@recyclemeorganictees.com
www.recyclemeorganictees.com
773 655 4210
"Clothing you can feel good about!"

Sara Diamond lives in Northern California. She is a Graduate Student in the Department of Entomology at the University of CA, Davis. Sara is working for a cleaner healthier environment and sustainable future.

Autumn Dibello is a third-grade recycler from Utah who wants to teach other kids how easy recycling can be.

Devon Green is the owner of 'Devon's Heal the World Recycling', which she began at age five. Her business includes giving of her time and raising funds to help others, as well as helping the planet. She is currently attending college in North Carolina.
Devonshealtheworld.com

Jessica Green is a sixth-grader and Vice President of Recycling for 'Devon's Heal the World' and Jessie too. She joined her sister's recycling business at the age of five. Jessica gives back to her community by raising money for those who can't help themselves.

Lynn Hasselburger is the mother of an eight-year-old boy and the owner of My Earth 360. In addition to teaching kids about the environment, she sells earth-friendly products such as reusable water bottles and cloth shopping bags.
myEARTH360.com
icountformyEARTH.com
blog.icountformyEARTH.com
shaklee.net/myEARTH/GetClean

Jake Henty is eleven years old and lives with his parents in St. Louis, Missouri. He teaches other kids how to create their own compost to cut down on waste and grow healthier gardens.
   His mother, Brenda Henty, owns a green business, My Green Boutique, www.mygreenboutique.com
p. 314.541.7279

brenda@mygreenboutique.com

Ryan Hreljac is the founder of Ryan's Well. Ryan has been providing fresh water wells for whole villages since he was only seven years old. The Hreljacs live in North Grenville, just south of Ottawa, Ontario, Canada. www.ryanswell.com

Janine Licare is from Manuel Antonio, Costa Rica. She co-founded Kids Saving the Rainforest when she was only nine years old, and is saving animal habitats and planting trees to make a cleaner, healthier world. Janine is currently a student at Stanford University. kidssavingtherainforest.com

Julie Mullin is the mother of one teenage son. She lives and teaches others to live a clean, sustainable life. Julie lives just south of Raleigh, North Carolina, in Wake County, where she runs a green business. **Fiberactive Organics, LLC**, www.fiberactiveorganics.com
919-772-412 fiberactive@earthlink.net
Saving the earth one stitch at a time.

Melissa Poe is the founder of Kids F.A.C.E.—Kids for a Clean Environment, created when she was only nine years old. Kids F.A.C.E., is the world's largest youth environmental organization. Melissa lives in Nashville, Tennessee. www.kidsface.com

St. Benedict School is a parochial school in the Archdiocese of Chicago. It is located in Blue Island, IL. The school has 175 students and serves preschool through grade eight, under the direction of Mrs. Susan Rys, principal. Students at St. Benedict have made a life-long commitment to service to the environment so that it is preserved for kids of the future. Visit our web page at www.stbenbi.org

Dotty Simmons is a grandmother from Dinsmore, California. Her family creates their own power and doesn't receive power from the main electrical grid. She is the owner of Simmons Natural Bodycare: Making Every Day Special
http://www.simmonsnaturals.com info@simmons-naturals.com
http://simmonsnaturals.blogspot.com
Working for a sustainable future

Emily Sikes is a fifteen-year-old from Arkansas and a member of 4-H, where she is learning and teaching others about environmental issues, including the reuse of household items.

Sara Sikes is a thirteen-year-old from Arkansas where she is setting an example for other kids and adults in using cloth bags to cut down on the waste of plastic.

Linda Stein is the mother of two and owner of the green cosmetics company: Zosimos Botanicals LLC, 28 Allenhurst Court Gaithersburg, MD 20878, linda@zosimosbotanicals.com , 1-877-889-9969 *Startup-Nation deems Zosimos Botanicals one of the Top 10 Greenest Home-Based Businesses of 2008. The 2nd Annual StartupNation Home-Based 100 contest ranked businesses in ten categories. The Greenest category applied to home-based businesses having a positive environmental and/or social impact.*

Jill A. Vanderwood is the author of four books for children, including: *What's It Like, Living Green? Kids Teaching Kids, by the Way They Live.* She has written this book to bring kids together to make a difference for the planet. www.throughtherug.com; www. jillvanderwood.com What's It Like, Living Green Blog: whatsitlikelivinggreen@blogger.com

Nicole Williams is a sixth-grade recycler from Utah who influences those around her to begin their own recycling program.

Caroll Wolverton lives in Florida. She is the author of seven books, including *Living Cheap and Loving it: tomatoes in the flower bed*.

Melissa Zenz is the mother of two from Florida who lives a dark green life, setting an example and letting her voice be heard in making changes for the earth and its creatures. Melissa is the owner of Kid Bean natural products.
KidBean.com - Vegan Family Superstore
http://www.kidbean.com
mzenz@kidbean.com

How Green Is My Family?

From the back cover
By Sara Diamond—Graduate Student, UC Davis
Find the category that fits you the best. Some families may be a combination of two categories.

White—this category is the absence of green
- You use paper or plastic bags for groceries
- Take long showers or fill up the bathtub
- Water the yard all day
- Always drive/ride in a car when you leave the house
- Leave lights, TV, and radio on when you leave a room
- Throw everything into the trash

Cactus Green
- You use paper and plastic bags grocery bags
- Enjoy long showers
- Sometimes water the yard during the day
- Sometimes take the bus or ride your bike, rather than driving/riding in a car
- Sometimes remember to turn off the lights, TV, or radio
- Put your recyclables into the curbside recycle bin

Prairie Green
- You have begun to take your own bags to the store
- Take short showers
- Always water the yard in the evening
- Sometimes ride your bike, walk or take public transportation
- Always turn out the lights, TV or radio when

leaving a room
•   Buy food in larger packages for less waste
•   Put your recyclables into the curbside recycle
bin

Grass Green
•   Always take your own bags to the store
•   Eat most of your meals at home, or take your
lunch to school—to prevent waste
•   Take short showers, and water your lawn only
in the evenings
•   Try to wear your clothes more than once, and
always wash full loads of laundry
•   Recycle aluminum cans for money
•   Use reusable water bottles, rather than buying
disposable bottles
•   Walk to school or take the bus, whenever pos-
sible

Leafy Green
•   All of Grass Green plus—recycle everything,
even if you need to take it to the recycle center
•   Use reusable rags for cleaning and earth
friendly cleaning products
•   Use cloth napkins, rags, and handkerchiefs
•   Grow some of your own herbs in a garden
•   Use recycled paper

Garden Green
•   All of Leafy Green plus—You seldom use your
car
•   You grow a garden and use organic compost,
fertilizers, and pest control
•   You have begun to compost
•   You teach others by the way you live

Moss Green
• All of Garden Green plus—You grow all you can in your garden
• You try to buy locally, to save on transport of food products
• You bottle your own fruit, or freeze your own vegetables, when possible
• You try to reuse clothing and find someone to use what you can't use

Forest Green
• All of Moss Green plus—You live off the land as much as you can
• You conserve power or use alternative power
• Your family drives a car with alternative fuel to reduce greenhouse gases
• You use water, power, food and paper responsibly and try to reuse, reduce, and recycle everything you can.
• You contribute little to the landfill, waste very little water or power, and add very little to the greenhouse gases.

About the Illustrator

Emma Austin is a seventeen-year-old artist who lives in sunny Queensland, Australia.

Emma loves animals; her family owns many pets including a Chihuahua named Pedro, a bearded Dragon named Mojo, and a cat named Soxy. Her family often cares for injured birds, as well.

Her love of animals has carried over into her artwork as she began drawing animals and things of nature ever since she could pick up a pencil. Emma started serious digital illustration in 2004.

Emma has taken art classes throughout her school years. Her artistic ability has led her to earn high marks for visual art in 2007 and 2008, receiving awards for both years.

After completing her final year of school, she hopes to achieve a Bachelor of Games Design and/or Illustration at Griffith University.

Jill Ammon Vanderwood is the winner of the Writer of the Year Award for 2008, presented by the League of Utah Writers. She was noted for her published works, as well as mentoring other writers, and community service to the Literacy Action Center, the Northwest Kiwanis Camp and the Wheelchair Foundation.

Jill participated in the first Earth Day celebration in Portland, Oregon. Now living in Utah, she is a mother and grandmother who wants to help the next generation work toward creating a healthier future for our planet.

Other books by Jill Ammon Vanderwood: Through the Rug; Through the Rug 2: Follow that Dog; and The San Francisco Adventures of Sara, the Pineapple Cat

Schools are invited to join the 'Green Leap for Literacy' campaign, free of charge. For information visit: www.jillvanderwood.com

Made in the USA